Donald Featherstone's Battle Notes for Wargamers

Solo Wargaming Edition

Edited by John Curry
With Arthur Harman

This first part of this book was first published in 1973 as *Battle Notes for Wargamers* by David & Charles Ltd. The original book has been supplemented by unpublished notes that were intended for a second edition that was never printed, and additional material added to each chapter detailing currently available figures and rules for the period, together with suggestions for further reading.

This edition printed 2010

Copyright © 2010 John Curry and Donald Featherstone

All rights reserved. No part of this book may be reproduced or transmitted in any form by any means, electronic, mechanical, photocopying, recording, or otherwise without the prior written permission of authors.

Books edited by John Curry as part of the History of Wargaming Project
Army Wargames: Staff College Exercises 1870-1980.
Charlie Wesencraft's Practical Wargaming
Charlie Wesencraft's With Pike and Musket
Donald Featherstone's Wargaming Airborne Operations
Donald Featherstone's Lost Tales
The Fred Jane Naval Wargame (1906) including the Royal Navy War Game (1921)
Paddy Griffith's Napoleonic Wargaming for Fun
Sprawling Wargames: Multi-player wargaming by Paddy Griffith
Verdy's 'Free Kriegspiel' including the Victorian Army's 1896 War Game
Tony Bath's Ancient Wargaming
Phil Dunn's Sea Battles
Peter Perla's The Art of Wargaming
And many others

See The History of Wargaming Project at www.wargaming.co for a continually expanding range of wargaming publications.

Front Cover: Battle of Guilford Courthouse, 15 March 1781, with General Nathaniel Greene observed as the veteran 1st Maryland Regiment threw back a British attack and countered with a bayonet charge. As they reformed their line, William Washington's Light Dragoons raced by to rescue raw troops of the 5th Maryland Regiment who had buckled under a furious assault of British Grenadiers and Guards.

ISBN 978-1-4467-3183-3

Foreword on Donald Featherstone's Battle Notes for Wargamers, Solo Wargaming Edition	5
Introduction	8
1. The Battle of Pharsalus	19
2. The Battle of Poitiers	28
3. The Battle of Barnet	37
4. The Battle of Cheriton	47
5. The Battle of Wynendael	57
6. The Battle of Prestonpans	66
7. The Battle of Guilford Courthouse	76
8. The Battle of Maida	87
9. The Battle of Aliwal	97
10. The Battle of Wilson's Creek	105
11. The Battle of the Little Big Horn	115
12. The Battle of Modder River	124
13. The ANZAC Landing at Gallipoli	135
14. The Raid on St Nazaire	143
15. The Attack on Pork Chop Hill	152
Appendix 1 Rules	163
Appendix 2 Terrain	165
Appendix 3 Website Addresses	167
Bibliography	169

Foreword on Donald Featherstone's Battle Notes for Wargamers, Solo Wargaming Edition

Donald Featherstone clearly spelt out his intentions for this book in the introductory chapter. The aim was to include sufficient information on selected battles which were small enough to be capable of being realistically represented on the wargame table without one figure representing a battalion.

The introductory chapter suggested ways of dealing with the 'imponderables' and surprise elements of every battle, the 'what if's', the flank marches and the sudden aberrations of previously sane commanders.

The fifteen battles described in separate chapters ranged from Pharsalus in the Roman Civil War (48 BC) to the battle for Pork Chop Hill in Korea (1953). A battle was selected from each key military period between them. Each battle was described as it happened and each commander involved was assessed on his performance on the day. What might have happened if the fortunes of war had been different was considered and ways of representing these chance factors were suggested. The problems of each commander and any special behavioural characteristics of the two forces such as high morale, treachery or downright stupidity were outlined. Each chapter concluded with a description of the battlefield, a scale drawing of a table-top representation and suggestions for modelling the terrain features. The appendices contained sources for rules and figures and a useful bibliography for those wanting more information. The original appendices with sources for rules and figures have not been included in this new edition, as they have been superseded by the passage of time, the proliferation of figures and options for rules, but notes at the end of each chapter list some suitable figures and rules for the benefit of readers who do not possess suitable armies and rules already, together with some suggestions for further reading.

The only criticism of the whole book could be the lack of detailed orders of battle; perhaps stating the number of units and their strengths, rather then the simple totals of each troop type, would have been more useful. As the book stood, readers could decide for themselves, dependent on what figures they had on their shelves, how many units of what strength they would deploy on the table top.

Don[1] is of the opinion that commanders were (and are) largely rational creatures. Their glaring mistakes uncovered by the uncompromising spotlight of history on their actions should always be balanced by consideration of why they acted as they did. This book attempts to suggest some of those reasons for the chosen battles included in this book.

---

[1] In conversation with the editor

Don also says that representing a particular battle on the table top is a fine exercise for a wargamer. The task includes studying the sources, finding battlefield maps, deciding what should be included on the tabletop terrain and what should not, the historically valid 'military possibilities' and *critically*, deciding what rule modifications are needed to create an accurate wargame of a particular battle. Whilst visiting wargaming shows, Don always found it more engaging to talk to people attempting to recreate a particular battle from the scrap book of history rather than those playing an imaginary or hypothetical battle 'typical' of the period.

This new edition of the original book came about by chance. One of the myths about Don is that everything he writes will always be published. It is not. Being an author consisted (and still does) of writing large amounts of material, some of which would get to print and some would not. In response to feedback, Don considered producing a second edition of the particularly well received *Battle Notes for Wargamers* by reformatting and editing the material to make it more accessible to the solo wargamer. While going though some thousands of pages of original material, the editor found a draft for the second edition.

Each battle includes most of the original book's material, but presented in a sequence to assist the solo wargamer. Each battle is now presented with a suggestion for the side the solo player should command.

The new sequence of the material is:

- Historical Background

- Description of the friendly forces

- Description of enemy forces

- The wargames terrain for the tabletop recreation.

- A prompt for the solo player to deploy their forces and write their orders before reading further.

- A description of the actual historical course of the battle.

- An outline of the enemy's orders.

- Ratings of the commanders and a discussion of the military possibilities, potential rule modifications and other factors contributing to surprise.

- The actual battlefield map

- Notes suggesting suitable wargame figures, rules and further reading for the particular campaign or battle

The reordering of the material, with the further suggestions by Don of historically valid orders for the enemy, should assist solo wargamers to recreate these battles. Don is not a fan of solo games; the companionship of like minded military enthusiasts is, for him, an inseparable part of the hobby. If, however, one is forced by circumstance to play solo games, then creating specific encounters from the past seems to Don to be a fine way to continue and enjoy one's hobby.

John Curry, Editor of the History of Wargaming Project
www.wargaming.co

Introduction

The idea of refighting the famous battles of history, reproducing Waterloo, Gettysburg, Alamein, etc, on the wargames table, is a most attractive proposition. Unfortunately it is almost impossible to put it into practice with any degree of realism. A significant part of the history of the world, these battles involved thousands of soldiers fighting over vast areas of ground. At the battle of Waterloo there were 100,000 French; 69,000 British, Dutch, Belgians and Germans, and more than 100,000 Prussians. Even drastically scaling down this number, so that 100 men on the battlefield approximate to one man on the wargames table, gives ludicrous infantry battalions of about seven or eight men, and the wargamer will still need about 3,000 model soldiers! Waterloo was a relatively small battle for the number of troops involved, yet it stretched across a frontage of about four miles and, even with a vastly reduced ground scale, an unreasonably large wargames table would be required to reconstruct it. The same applies to Gettysburg, and, considering that Alamein was fought over 138 mile front over eleven days, the almost insurmountable difficulties of recreating major battles can be appreciated.

However, military history abounds with conflicts that are highly suitable for reproduction on the wargames table - battles involving small numbers, so that realistic scaling down is possible. This is important because, if the battle is to bear anything more than a titular resemblance to the original, the table top armies must be an accurate representation of the original forces, both in their comparative numbers and in their composition of troop types. It is possible in the battles described later for one man on the wargames table to equal as few as five men in real life, and some battles, such as Pork Chop Hill, can be fought on a man-for-man basis. The size and topographical features of the historical battlefield must lend themselves to reproduction on the wargames table, and all those considered in this book are suitable in area and frontage for this purpose. Each battle also possesses tactical and human interests that make it worthy of simulation.

Table-top reconstructions of an historical battle must conform as closely as possible, to the events that occurred on the battlefield itself. It is pointless to construct a terrain resembling the battlefield of Maida, for example, and then let loose upon it a host of infantry, cavalry and artillery whose general milling about bears no relation to the original conflict. Every aspect of the battle has to be considered in its correct context, and in chronological order, so that it can be simulated and affected by the fluctuations and fortunes of war, without radically departing from the Military Possibilities of the day. The wargamer should consider what might have occurred in conjunction with what did occur.

It is doubtful whether wargames will ever give one profound military insight[2], but the wargamer may gain an understanding of the problems of the commanders in the field and a glimpse of the military thinking of the time by relighting each battle in the correct tactical manner, using the formations and weapons of the day. The purpose of this book is to discuss these factors and to suggest practical methods of simulation that will produce an accurate, realistic and enjoyable wargame of the original battle. From the point of view of wargaming purely and simply, the battles described can be transported with magical ease backwards or forwards in time, so that the terrain and situation at Pharsalus in 48 BC, for instance, can be used by Wellington's seasoned Peninsular troops, or the rugged country around the Little Big Horn can be labelled 'A Tract of the North-West Frontier of India' and Custer replaced by one of Queen Victoria's commanders.

To refight any historical battle realistically, the terrain must closely resemble both in scale and appearance the area over which the original conflict raged, and the troops accurately represent the original forces. The most obvious manner of the battle is for the troops to perform precisely the same manoeuvres as they did in the past, take the same percentage of losses and achieve the same success or failure. This is an historical exercise, not a wargame, and will only serve as a demonstration of what occurred during the real-life battle. It is the manner in which public demonstrations of the Battle of Hastings were carried out by the author during that town's 900th anniversary celebrations[3].

Another method is to follow the original course of events reasonably well, but allow some leeway, without too much imaginative stretch, for a reversed result. Too many liberties may not be taken, however, or, as we have said, the battle will become a wargame played for its own sake, lacking any precision. We must not allow the opposing table-top generals the advantage of hindsight, so that they can perform tactical manoeuvres far in advance of those known to their counterparts on the historical battlefield. In a wargame between Ancient Britons and Romans, for example, the commander of the former would be most unlikely to throw his entire force forward in the characteristic headlong charge favoured by the Britons because he would know that it would be repulsed by the disciplined formation and tactics of the Romans. The real chieftain, however, would not have conceived a tactical plan that included feint attacks, outflanking movements, feigned withdrawals to destroy Roman cohesion or

---

[2] However, Don and Paddy Griffith used model soldiers to portray contemporary descriptions of British responses to French attacks in the Peninsular War, which helped Paddy produce the analysis of British tactics in *Forward Into Battle* that contradicted Oman's hitherto largely unquestioned 'firepower' explanation of British success, and is now widely accepted.

[3] See Chapter 12 of *War Game Campaigns* by Donald Featherstone, reprinted in the History of Wargaming Project

holding back a reserve; for his woad-covered Britons would never have obeyed orders with the discipline and steadiness of the Grenadier Guards. The wargamer should remember the tactical limitations of his troops, therefore, or we shall find, if the commander of the Ancient Britons is more conversant with table-top tactics than his Roman counterpart, that the semi-savage Britons are being handled in a tactical fashion superior to the well trained and highly disciplined Romans.

It is essential, therefore, that the tactics and formations of the original battle are reproduced and that all troops are obliged to conform to their known standard methods of fighting. For example, at Pharsalus the Roman legion formed up its ten cohorts three-deep on a frontage of 2,000 ft, so allowing each legionary six feet of space in which to fight. On the flanks and in front the auxiliary slingers and archers skirmished and flung their missiles. Following the cardinal rule of dealing with an enemy on the defensive, Caesar's legions began their attack when 120 yards away, with the front line of cohorts moving forward at the march and then at the double until the first two ranks of each cohort were about 60 yards from the enemy. Then they launched themselves forward and hurled their *pila* at a range of about twenty paces; their comrades followed up and repeated the performance until the back lines of the cohorts had thrown their *pila* over the heads of their front ranks, which were now among the enemy, thrusting murderously with their short swords. They fought for exactly fifteen minutes before being withdrawn and a fresh century or cohort thrown in. At the same time, the second line of cohorts moved forward, their front men preparing for their sixty yard run. The third line of cohorts was held in reserve to mop up the last of the enemy resistance or to cover a retreat if necessary. In reconstructing the battle of Pharsalus, therefore, the wargamer should employ these tactics.

It is important also to read varying accounts of a battle and the events leading up to it beforehand, because therein may lie any number of factors influencing its trend and pattern. Perhaps bad weather or muddy roads caused a significant proportion of one army to be late or to fail to arrive on the battlefield at all. Consideration of the campaign reveals the objective of the battle, such as the Black Prince attempting to join with an ally or to return home with the booty of the expedition, but being forced to fight at Poitiers. Armed with knowledge of a commander's historical intentions, one may better understand his tactical plans. One may vary the objective on the wargames table: for example, at the Little Big Horn Custer may try to fight his way back to join Reno instead of pressing forward to destroy an Indian force which, unknown to him, is overwhelmingly superior in numbers to his own.

Primed with background reading, the wargamer should now analyse the battle, seeking those moves that led to victory or defeat. Each phase should be considered carefully, while seeking possible alternatives to the historical trend of events. These alternatives will be called Military Possibilities, which may be defined by reference to Custer above. If he had joined Reno, what would have happened?

Would their combined force have been able to hold out? You may find out on the wargames table.

The wargamer can enter the brains of Julius Caesar, the Black Prince, Marlborough, Sir Harry Smith, Lyon at Wilson's Creek, the ill-fated General George Custer, and Sir Paul Methuen at Modder River. He can win a VC with Newman at St Nazaire, and grapple with the problems of a brave lieutenant like Clemons on Pork Chop Hill.

Over and above the normal provisions of conventional wargames rules, certain factors must receive emphasis if an accurate and realistic simulation is to be achieved. Frequent references to these factors will be encountered in the various battle reconstructions that follow, and they are considered herewith in greater detail.

Military Possibilities

Military Possibilities are controlled and logical alternative courses of action that, had they been taken at the appropriate time during the battle, might well have caused a complete reversal of the result. Courses of action followed by opposing wargamers with the agreement of both, Military Possibilities are neither excuses for indulging in whims and fancies, nor for diverting events merely 'to see what happens'. In some cases the course of action indicated by a Military Possibility results in a more reasonable and credible result than occurred on the field of conflict.

Some Military Possibilities might depend on Luck, represented by the throw of a die or the turn of a Chance Card, the simplest means of simulating the ebb and flow of war.

It must be decided whether Military Possibilities are to radically alter the historical course of the battle or be restricted to relatively minor aspects of it, when they may result in a more interesting 'twist' in tactics, or even influence the eventual outcome.

Numerous Military Possibilities are included in the simulation advice and suggestions that accompany each battle; such as at Cheriton, where the young and impetuous Royalist cavalry commander, Sir Henry Bard, is made to resist his impulse to attack the Roundhead cavalry, so forcing Waller either to attack the Royalists in their strong defensive position or to withdraw from the field. Another allows the Coldstream Guards to ford the Riet River during the early stages of the battle of Modder River in 1899, when they could have taken the Boer position in reverse. Military Possibilities abound in all battles; the interest and colour they bring to the wargames table are proportionate to the ingenuity of the wargamer.

Ratings of Commanders

No wargamer likes to follow rigidly a course of action that history tells him will bring defeat, particularly when he has a marked numerical superiority, so, to save his face in such a situation, the original commander may be classified as 'average' or 'below average'.

If both forces are equal in strength, morale, equipment, position, manoeuvrability, etc, victory will almost certainly go to the better commander. In many of the battles described in this book a strong enemy force has been defeated by a numerically weaker army solely because its commander possessed outstanding tactical ability and was capable of inspiring his men to exceptional heights or, lacking either of those qualities, he just happened to be better than his opposing commander. Thus, just as history dictates that one commander was 'exceptional' while his opponent was only 'average' or 'below average', so this fact has to be reflected on the wargames table.

Taking the Battle of Poitiers as an example, the Black Prince must be classified as an 'above average' commander, as might be Warwick, Salisbury and even the Captal de Buch. The French King, the Dauphin and the Duke of Orleans must be classed as 'below average' commanders, while one of the two marshals, Clermont or Audrehen, can be an 'above average' commander.

The effect upon the battle of a commander's rating must be reflected by his troops, since those of an 'above average' commander will possess a higher standard of morale and better fighting qualities — represented by adding 1 (or any pre-decided score) to any dice affecting morale or fighting qualities. Conversely, a 'below average' commander would deduct 1 from dice scores, and the troops of an 'average' commander would remain unaffected.

An 'above average' commander could be given greater flexibility of movement and, within certain limits, the ability to undertake tactical movements outside his period (in other words, the wargamer is allowed to be himself). With certain reservations, the 'average' commander can be given the ability to alter characteristic fighting patterns, controlling and manoeuvring his force as suggested by their 'Style of Fighting' (explained in the *War Games through the Ages*[4] series). The 'below average' commander is given no such opportunity, and must control and manoeuvre his force without deviating from their 'Style of Fighting' whatsoever.

If a system is used where, at the start of the battle, orders have to be written for each army or group, the grading of commanders can be reflected by ruling that those armies or groups under 'below average' commanders must conform rigidly to their initial orders until they are disorganised by a forced reaction (such as failing a morale test). 'Average' commanders can write orders to carry through three moves of the game; at the conclusion of the third move fresh orders may be written if circumstances have not already altered the original instructions. 'Above average' commanders may write orders at the beginning of each move of the game.

---

[4] *War Games Through the Ages*, Donald Featherstone, Stanley Paul, 1973-6; *Volume 1: 3000 BC to 1500 AD; Volume 2: 1420 to 1783; Volume 3: 1792-1859; Volume 4: 1861 to 1945*

An alternative is to allow all commanders, whatever their rating, to write their orders at the beginning of the game, but the lower the commander's grade, the greater number of moves he must take before he alters his orders, while the 'above average' commander may change his instructions much more rapidly.

With the exception of Julius Caesar at Pharsalus, there was no historically 'outstanding' leader present at any of the battles described in this book, so that the rating of commanders must be by 'local' comparison, and the reconstruction notes for each battle include a suggested rating for them. However, because an 'above average' rating is given to Lord George Murray at Prestonpans, it does not imply that he was a commander of the same calibre as Caesar himself. Nor should chauvinism cause American readers to feel aggrieved because George Custer is rated 'below average' at Little Big Horn — the rating is solely on his tactical ability and does not reflect upon his courage. In passing, it is interesting to note that most 'below average' commanders were men of great personal courage, such as Custer, Sir Hugh Gough or Lord Methuen - perhaps bravery was bestowed upon them to compensate for marked deficiencies in other qualities.

Chance Cards

Chance Cards introduce pleasant and unpleasant factors that materially affect aspects of a battle, perhaps even its result. They pose eventualities — tactical, physiological or psychological — and the commander drawing such a card has to take practical steps to carry out the instructions it bears.

Each historical battle could have its own set of cards designed to cover eventualities likely in such a situation. Closely allied to Military Possibilities, Chance Cards form the 'human' element that may affect the purely tactical aspects of a Military Possibility. Chance Cards can affect such aspects as de Buch's flank attack on the French at Poitiers by setting obstacles in his way (see Chapter 2). Machiavellian umpires often draw the countryside in such a manner as to present unexpected obstacles.

Every battle of military history abounds with situations which, in wargames, could give rise to the use of Chance Cards. The fifteen engagements described in this book possess their share — the more obvious are listed but many more will spring to the mind of the imaginative wargamer.

Time Charts

Most of our battles include some 'surprise factor' that needs recording, so that a check can be kept, for example, on the anticipated time of arrival of a flanking force. A Time Chart programmes such vital factors beyond dispute. The Chart must include those manoeuvres whose timing is an important feature of the battle; each of them, or stages in their accomplishment, should be treated as a move in the game.

A Time Chart is vital in keeping check on off-table moves on a map, where different forces are moving along various routes or attempting outflanking movements that will bring troops on to the table-top battlefield at some intermediate stage in the conflict. It is almost impossible to retain control of such factors without a Time Chart.

Keeping in touch with detached portions of a force might require their commander, perhaps unaware of their exact location, sending messengers, whose progress must be recorded on the Time Chart. Thus, the messengers' exact time of arrival is known, and the unit to whom they are bringing orders cannot react until those orders are received. The non-arrival or delay of orders provides Military Possibilities that can realistically alter the course of a historical conflict.

As an example, consider the longest battle in the book — the CCF attack on Pork Chop Hill. This Time Chart will need to begin at about 2200 hours on 16 April 1953, and last through that night, and all through the following day and night, until after sunset on 18 April. On the other hand, at Prestonpans, scarcely more than five minutes elapsed from the first onslaught on Cope's army to the breaking of his entire front line. But the Time Chart must start when Cope took up position on the higher ground around Tranent, so that it gives full scope for charting the Highlanders' outflanking movement, and allows for their possible discovery and interception at the Riggonhead defile. Then follows Cope's realisation of the new threat and his redeployment to face it; the Highland onslaught, and the speedy rout of the royal army. In this case, the amount of time taken by each game-move will need to be short.

Simulation of Surprise

Every one of the battles described herein was affected by the element of surprise. While victory frequently goes to the big battalions, it can also be vastly influenced by shrewd tactical moves or the mere fluctuations of fortune. Surprise movements of bodies of troops, so that they suddenly arrive upon the rear or flank of the unsuspecting enemy (as at Prestonpans), are difficult to simulate on the wargames table, but such movements charted on a map enable forces to be manoeuvred so that the enemy is unaware of their intention, and even their existence, until contact is made.

The scale of 1 to 12 is used for all terrain maps in this book, so that a wargames table 8 feet by 5 feet appears 8 inches by 5 inches on the map. Draw a map 24 inches long by 15 inches wide, which will cover an area of nine wargames tables, with the battleground taking up the middle rectangle. Then, in the surrounding rectangles, continue topographical features such as hills, rivers, roads, etc. Cover the map with a pattern of inch squares, by drawing fine lines with a mapping pen on the surface of the map, or else by laying upon it a transparent plastic sheet upon which such squares have been marked.

Movement on this map is to the same scale as movement on the table, so that infantry moving 12 inches on the wargames table will move 1 inch on the map; this is most important, because it is the means by which 'off-the-table' movements are made. To illustrate the practical use of this map, combined with the Time Chart, let us take the Battle of Barnet. Oxford's force chased Hastings's men off the wargames table and on to the larger area of the map as far as the village of Barnet itself, moving at an agreed speed (according to the rules) over the specified distance. Time (in the form of game-moves) will be taken up by:

(a) the pursuit,
(b) Oxford rallying his force and halting the pursuit, and
(c) his force's return to the battlefield (the table), where it strikes Montagu in the flank by mistake.

During this period the battle in the centre oblong will have been proceeding. Oxford's movements are known to both wargames commanders, but a degree of uncertainty can be introduced by considering certain Military Possibilities. The distance of the pursuit can be varied, for instance, so that it will take Oxford a greater or lesser time to pursue Hastings, and bring him back to the main battle earlier or later than anticipated.

Surprise is difficult to simulate in the reconstruction of a historical battle, but if the conflict is to be accurately reproduced the surprise *must* appear. However, it can be tempered by Military Possibilities arising from local rules, morale factors or other means suggested in this section. Although all the troops are in full view on the table-top, a certain degree of tactical surprise and apparent concealment is made possible by each commander initially drawing up a plan of the tactics he intends to use, giving a broad outline of the role to be played by each unit of his army. Both commanders have eight playing cards, two being aces. Before each move a card is drawn, and the commander may alter a unit's allotted role if he draws an ace, but, if not, he is committed to his original plan. This method can be used in conjunction with the ratings of commanders, simulating the decisiveness of De la Rey and the 'woolliness' of Methuen at Modder River by giving the British one ace and the Boers three aces per eight cards.

The flank attack by the Gascon Captal de Buch at Poitiers causes certain practical problems on the wargames table. In 1356 the French had no idea that this attack was coming in on their left flank, whereas in a reconstruction they will be fully aware of the daunting fact. The English commander may be given the choice of sending de Buch out to his right or to his left, so that the French, while being aware of the flank attack, will not know from which side they are threatened. But they must take steps to counter it by allocating men to watch the flanks of their column, and these men will not count in the main mêlée.

Chance Cards and Military Possibilities may well cause the flanking force to be so delayed that it will never arrive at all or be too late to affect the result of the mêlée.

The countryside surrounding the area of the battle (in the centre rectangle) can be drawn inaccurately on the map of the commander who is due to be surprised, so that he is unable to estimate the possibilities of an outflanking movement or the time it will take to reach him. On the other hand, the commander of the outflanking side can be given an inaccurate map, a Military Possibility that will affect his surprise move and give the original loser a slight chance of reversing the decision. If such steps are taken, it is advisable to have an umpire with an accurate map, for that will save a lot of arguments.

A reasonably successful method of surprise and concealment, again using maps that can be as accurate or inaccurate as desired, requires the commander making the surprise move to work out, on a scaled map, the number of game-moves that it will take. He writes down:

(a) the unit or units involved (or total strength of force),
(b) the route from A to B (starting point of move to point of contact), and
(c) the number of moves required.

If the force making the surprise move was visible in the battle, it will remain on the wargames table and will not move until the game-move in which it strikes home. If it was *not* visible to the enemy, it will move exclusively on the map, to be revealed and placed on the table when its presence was discovered. Using written movement orders (described in Chapter 2 of *Advanced Wargames*[5]) and with a scaled map of the terrain, the commander perpetrating the surprise plots it for the required number of game-moves, writing instructions in progressive columns. On the completion of the requisite number of moves, the surprise force is disclosed by the wargamer controlling it. He must declare if he wishes to terminate his concealed move before its completion, when he must move his troops up to the point they have reached. Surprise is then considered to have been lost, even if his troops are now technically concealed. A suspicious enemy commander may challenge, but his suspicions will need to be reasonably precise, as to direction and intention — the advisability of using an umpire is stressed. In the event of something happening on the wargames table that interferes with the surprise move, such as an enemy force crossing or positioning itself on the line of march, the move will have to be revealed and a decision taken as to which side is more surprised. This eventuality could take the form of a Military Possibility.

---

[5] Reprinted as part of the History of Wargaming Project

Another method of simulating a concealed force requires each commander to have a set of eight or ten progressively numbered terrain maps, drawn on tracing paper. At the start of the battle each commander draws on his No 1 map blocks representing his troops at their agreed starting point and, from each block, draws an arrow indicating his first move in scaled move-distances. The umpire holds one map over the other to see whether or not any troops are within visual distance of each other or have come into contact. Each commander then places his No 2 over his No 1 map and draws blocks over the ends of the arrows indicating the first move, before drawing in the arrow representing his second move. The umpire checks both maps and marks on each the position of any enemy forces that can be seen. The procedure carries on with progressively numbered maps until a contact is made; then the troops are placed upon the wargames table, having approached each other as through the smoke of a battlefield.

Perhaps the simplest way of achieving surprise is for the host not to tell the visiting player the name of the battle he is fighting. For example, without mentioning the name of the battle the host could give the visitor the story of the events leading up to Cope's army forming up and facing south at Prestonpans, a course the visitor follows on the wargames table only to find, as did Cope, that the Highlanders have suddenly arrived on his left flank. An obvious snag to this procedure is that the host will not be able to take a leading part in the battle but may have to be umpire or hold a subordinate role under one or other of the commanders. If the host is arranging a battle to be fought between two other wargamers, the relative insignificance of the battles described in this book may mean that one or both contestants have little idea of what occurred.

Morale

Morale concerns the discipline and confidence of troops, both collectively and individually, and was believed by Napoleon to be three times as important as physical factors. In at least twelve of the fifteen battles described later the morale of the troops played a major part in deciding the outcome of the battle. Thus, there must be adequate simulation of this intangible factor, which causes men suddenly to break, or to rally and beat a force much larger than themselves, in spite of being attacked in flank or rear and having lost their officers. The Battle of Guilford Courthouse is an excellent example of such conduct.

The reasons behind a soldier's fear or exaltation have not changed since the beginnings of time. The hail of arrows from the English archers at Poitiers in 1356 aroused the same consternation and wavering among the French as did the grenades thrown by the CCF on Pork Chop Hill in 1953. Thus, there will be a basic resemblance in morale rules for all periods, though aspects peculiar to various ages must be considered.

A familiar wargames method of allowing a smaller force some chance of success is to use morale rules that cause their numerically superior but otherwise inferior opponents to break and run, often before or at minimum contact. This factor is suggested as the best method of simulating Sir Harry Smith's success at Aliwal.

Artillery

Modern guns are too long-ranged to allow them to be placed on the wargames table with the enemy upon whom they are firing. In the battles of Modder River, Gallipoli and Pork Chop Hill, for instance, artillery fire is simulated by 'off-table map-shoots', which are carried out by marking the guns on a map such as those already mentioned and then concealing a figure (an observer) on the wargames table to lay the guns on to the targets he can see. To register a nominated aiming point, the observer must make a dice score of 5 or 6, which means that a hit is registered on that point (marked by a counter). Three such aiming points may be held at any one time. The observer may bring fire on to them unless the gun he is spotting for has moved (when it must be completely re-registered). The aiming points are also lost if an observer is killed. Guns may extend their target area by the observer nominating an aiming point and then altering the position of the 'Burst Pattern', providing a part of the pattern is still touching that point. A 'Burst Pattern' is a six inch square of transparent plastic with four 2 inch diameter circles numbered 1, 2, 3 and 4; the pattern bears a painted arrow which must point directly towards the firing gun. To simulate a shell burst, a pin is pushed through a centre hole in the 'Burst Pattern' into the 'hit' counter; the pattern laid, arrow directed towards the gun, and a dice score of 1 to 4 indicates the destruction of anything in that specifically numbered circle. A dice score of 5 or 6 indicates the shell has buried itself in the ground without exploding.

Artillery firing without an observer requires the map of the table to be divided into a grid of 12 inch by 12 inch squares, each of them being again gridded into six 2 inch squares, numbered 1-6. The firer nominates the large square, and a dice throw indicates the small square into the centre of which the 'Burst Pattern' pin is pushed. A further dice throw reveals the point of the shell burst. Details of 'off-table map-shoots' are given in Chapter 5 of *Advanced Wargames*[6].

---

[6] Reprinted as part of the History of Wargaming Project

1. The Battle of Pharsalus

9 August 48 BC

You are Julius Caesar[7] facing Pompey[8] in the potentially decisive battle of the Roman Civil War.

Historical Background

AT THIS stage of the Roman Civil War (50 to 44 BC) both armies were manoeuvring in Macedonia; after a reverse at Dyrrachium, Caesar had retreated 200 miles south-west into Thessaly, with Pompey's larger force cautiously following. Both armies camped on opposite sides of the Plain of Pharsalus, as Caesar regrouped and was reinforced by the troops of Domitius Calvinus while Pompey's army was strengthened by the legion of Metellus Pius Scipio; the men of both armies were irritable and pressing for a decisive action. On 9 August 48 BC (in modern dating), Pompey decided to risk an attempt to overwhelm Caesar's numerically inferior force,

Friendly Forces

With only 30,000 infantry and 1,000 cavalry, Caesar formed his tough and dedicated legions[9] into the customary three lines, extending the intervals between cohorts to match the frontage of Pompey's army; his third line acted as a reserve. Caesar held back and took personal command of six[10] cohorts (about 2,000 men) to cover his right rear and support his cavalry. His left flank rested securely on the steep bank of the Enipeus River.

---

[7] Gaius Iulius Caesar (100BC-44BC), nephew of Gaius Marius, reformer of the Roman Army, successful general and member – with Pompey and Crassus – of the Triumvirate which controlled Rome prior to Crassus's death, which precipitated a power struggle - the Civil War – with Pompey.

[8] Gnaeus Pompeius Magnus – Pompey 'the Great' – (106BC-48BC), made his name by defeating Domitianus Ahenobarbus in Africa, had married Caesar's daughter Iulia and had been a member of the Triumvirate before the death of Crassus.

[9] On the left, Marcus Antonius commanded Legion VII and the combined Legions VIII and IX; in the centre, Calvinus had Legion VI, with a new legion on each flank; on the right, Sulla had Legions X, XI and XII, numbering 82 understrength cohorts in total.

[10] More recently published accounts, listed in the Notes at the end of this chapter, state that Caesar detached one cohort from the third line of each of his eight legions to form this mobile reserve.

Enemy Forces

Pompey formed line-of-battle on the plain between the opposing camps; his force totalled 60,000 infantry[11] and 7,000 cavalry. The cavalry on the right wing were supported by light infantry (archers and slingers).

Pompey's legionaries were commanded by Metellus Pius Scipio[12] while his cavalry were led by Titus Labienus. Caesar's left wing was commanded by Mark Antony; his centre by Domitius Calvinus and his right wing by Publius Sulla.

---

[11] Pompey had elements of twelve legions and seven Spanish cohorts. On Pompey's left flank, Lentulus commanded auxiliaries, the Spanish cohorts and the Cicilian legion; on the right, under Ahenobarbus, were Legions I and III.

[12] According to Goldsworthy and Warry, Scipio commanded the centre; the left was commanded by Lentulus [Warry] or Afranius [Goldsworthy].

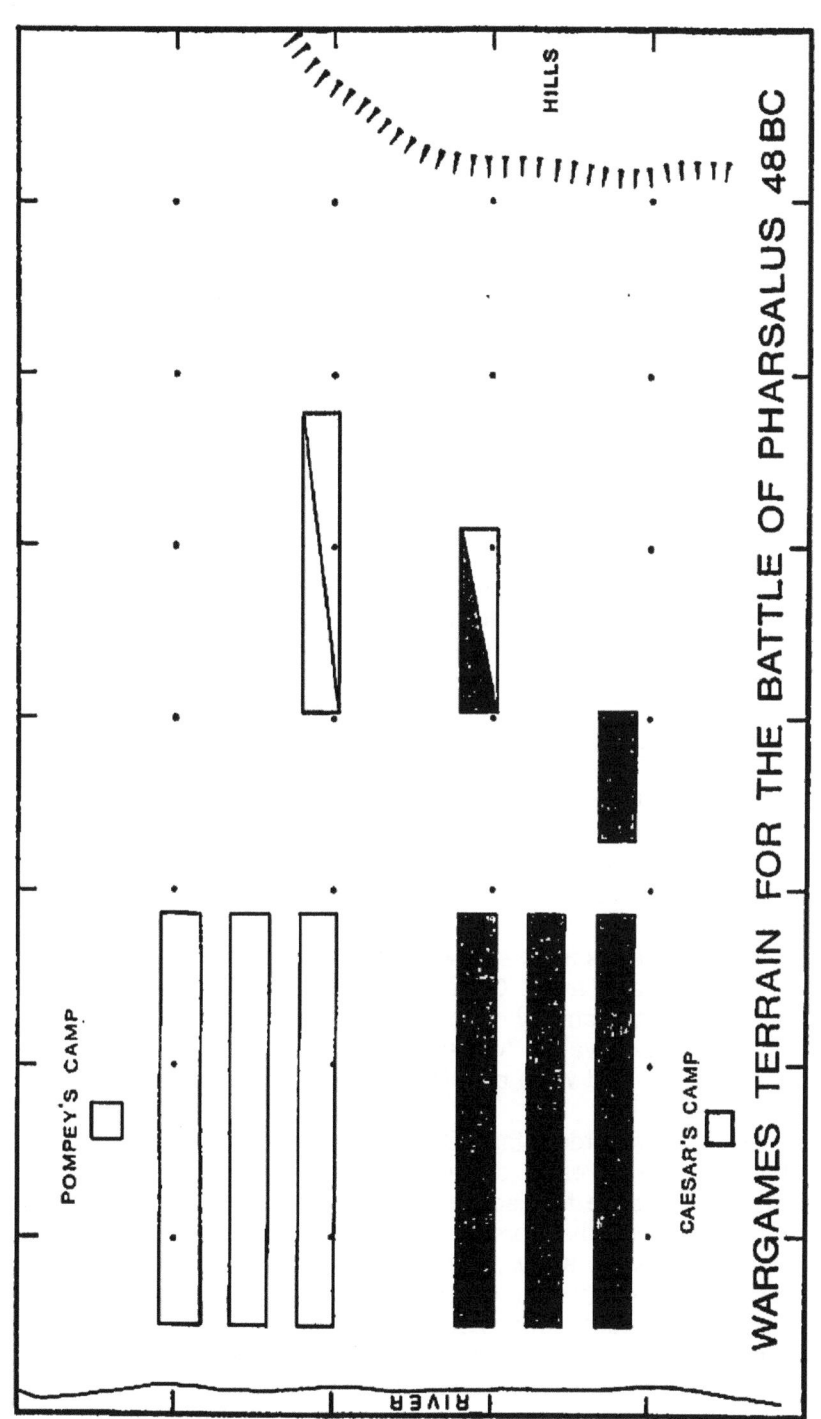

Construction of Terrain

This battle was fought on a perfectly flat plain, so that any wargames table or flat surface will suffice, though, for the sake of colour and interest, patches of scrub could be dotted over the terrain, with small groups of rocks, etc. Caesar faces north and Pompey faces south, with the arena bordered on the west by the river and on the east by the hills.

Stop! Read no further until you have deployed the forces and issued your detailed written orders.

The course of the actual historical battle.

At this time the normal Roman formation had the infantry in the centre and the cavalry on the wings to prevent the centre from being out flanked. Once the battle got under way and the enemy started to retreat, the cavalry moved forward and cut them down, so the main fighting was done by the infantry with the horsemen as a secondary force. Pharsalus was a notable exception because Pompey, having a seven to one superiority in this arm, used his horsemen as shock troops against Caesar's right wing; otherwise Pompey was uncharacteristically lethargic and relied on a tactical plan based on his superior numbers and his strong cavalry force, placed on the left to make an outflanking movement.

As soon as his dispositions were completed, Caesar ordered his first two lines of infantry to advance and attack Pompey's motionless army; on his immediate right flank he posted his small force of cavalry. To steady his troops, who lacked battle experience, and calculating that it would make his flank attack more effective, Pompey ordered his troops to stand and await Caesar's attack. As the lines of infantry clashed together, Pompey launched his large force of horsemen against Caesar's cavalry. Although greatly outnumbered, the latter fought stubbornly and were only forced back by sheer weight of numbers.

It has been recorded that Caesar had trained a force of light infantrymen, one to each cavalryman, to work together in mutual protection so that the foot soldiers protected the horsemen who had been unseated and the horsemen protected the infantry when they were under pressure. Knowing that Pompey's horsemen were young and inexperienced, Caesar ordered his light infantry to thrust their javelins upwards into the faces of the horsemen, causing them to draw away in disorder. Although they were forced back, Caesar's cavalry played their part in pinning down the enemy's numerically superior force until, at the decisive moment, Caesar personally led his selected reserve of six cohorts against the flank of Pompey's horsemen.

The experienced legionaries scattered the surprised cavalry before them, then pushed on to slaughter some light infantry (archers and slingers) who were following them up, before turning against the left flank of Pompey's main army, which was heavily engaged with Caesar's two lines of legionaries. Leaving the six cohorts he had just led to victory, Caesar galloped to join his third line of infantry, to lead them through the intervals of the first two lines and smash into the front of the now exhausted Pompeian legions. Deserted by their cavalry, overwhelmingly assailed in front and flank by Caesar's legions, the Pompeian troops broke and fled.

Without halting his victorious troops, Caesar pursued the fleeing army to storm the enemy camp and, without letting his men stop to plunder, pursued the fugitives until they dispersed in all directions. Pompey fled and embarked on a vessel for Egypt, where he was murdered shortly afterwards.

In this decisive battle Caesar lost 200 legionaries and 30 centurions, together with about 2,000 wounded. Pompey lost 15,000 killed and wounded, and 24,000 of his men were taken prisoner.

The numbers involved here are larger than for any other battle in the book, but this is unimportant as long as the wargamer uses the number of cohorts employed in the historical battle (their table-top size and strength are immaterial). Because of the ready availability of Roman soldiers in plastic or metal, in a variety of scales, this battle is most suitable for reproduction by groups of wargamers, each supplying his own Roman forces.

An outline of the enemy's orders.

At the start of the battle: roll one die: on a score of 1-5 Pompey's infantry may not move until attacked; 6 – the army charges if Caesar's force is within a charge move. Roll one die: on a score of 1-3 Pompey's cavalry charges and attempts to contact the enemy cavalry; 4-6 - they may not move, until the enemy cavalry are within charging distance.

Pompey's army should follow standard Roman tactics of attacking with the first line, then the second, then the third, but as their commander is below average, they should be slow to respond to developments in the battle.

Ratings of the Commanders and Military Possibilities

Julius Caesar must of course be 'above average' while, on the day, it would seem that his experienced opponent Pompey should be classified as 'below average', as should his cavalry commander Titus Labienus. Of Caesar's subordinates—Mark Antony, Domitius Calvinus and Publius Sulla — the first named is said to have performed very creditably, and together they can be classified as 'average', as can Pompey's other subordinate, Metellus Pius Scipio.

The prime consideration in the reconstruction is to balance up the considerable numerical differences between the troops, by means of Caesar's superior rating and his actions, first with cohorts and then with his third line, and this balancing may be done by giving all his troops superior morale and fighting ability ratings. Their fighting ability is illustrated by the exploits of Caesar's infantry, who, though fewer in numbers, showed themselves to be tougher and more experienced than Pompey's.

The battle will start without any manoeuvring, with Pompey's motionless formations being attacked by Caesar's first and second lines. By not moving forward, Pompey's formations of infantry failed to blunt the impact of Caesar's legions, giving the latter a bonus in the resulting mêlée. A Military Possibility can be evoked here by allowing Pompey's men, in fact, to move forward, though that may tip the odds too far against Caesar's numerically weaker forces.

Outnumbered seven to one by Pompey's cavalry, Caesar's horsemen must have fought bravely. However, since few wargames rules will allow any force to stand against such disproportionate odds, several Military Possibilities can be used: Caesar's cavalry can charge forward, so blunting the force of the attack, and the light infantry can be allowed to send a shower of missiles at Pompey's onrushing cavalry, causing them casualties that will necessitate them taking a morale test before making contact. It may well be that one or more of their squadrons are turned back, so reducing the odds against Caesar's smaller force. Obviously such a large force would not all come into action at once, and their fighting frontage would match that of their lesser enemy. This would mean that a large proportion of their force stretched back beyond the mêlée, with a large extent of exposed flank, into which Caesar personally led his six cohorts, with devastating effect.

A Military Possibility here could allow the outermost ranks of Pompey's cavalry to see the oncoming legionaries and to turn and meet them. But this would so distort a vital aspect of the battle as to place it beyond realism. A practical means of simulating Caesar's surprise attack can be chosen from suggestions in the 'Surprise' section

So important was Caesar's leading his third line of legionaries through the intervals of his first two lines to deliver a final blow to Pompey's infantry that it must be given special consideration, and can involve a number of Military Possibilities. For example, it could be decided that Caesar was too much involved with his infantry attack on the Pompeian cavalry to leave them, though as he did leave them, one might allow a drop in their morale after his departure. Another Military Possibility is to let the third line of infantry make their attack before Caesar joins them, and to see what happens to them without his personal leadership.

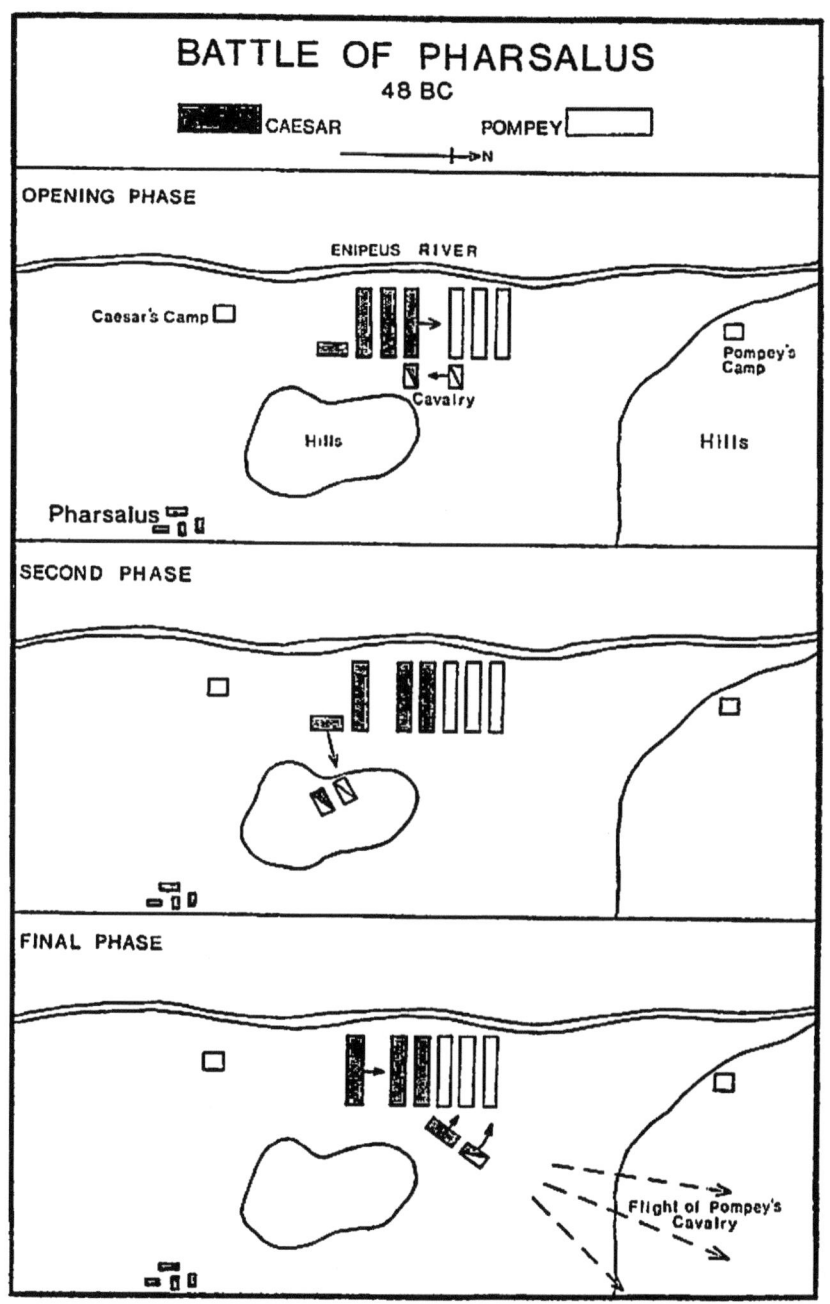

Notes

These notes – and those to the other chapters – are not exhaustive lists of all the suitable figures, rules and books that are available, and only figures manufactured and/or sold in the United Kingdom are listed. Website, rather than postal, addresses, will be found in Appendix to save unnecessary repetition.

Figures suitable for Pharsalus

For Pharsalus, a battle involving relatively large forces, wargamers who do not already possess suitable figures will probably prefer to use smaller scale models, so no listing of 25/28mm figures has been given.

2mm
Irregular Miniatures have Republican/early Imperial legionaries and other suitable troops.

6mm or 1/300 scale
Baccus has Marian legionaries in its Republican Roman range, or its Imperial auxiliaries could be used instead.
Heroics and Ros have Caesar's Legions.
Rapier Miniatures have Republican Romans.

10mm
Magister Militum has Marian Romans.
Old Glory UK Grand Scale has a Caesar's Gallic Wars range.
Pendraken has Republican Romans.

15mm
Essex Miniatures have Marian Romans.
FreiKorp 15 has Caesarian Romans in its Ancients ranges.
Irregular Miniatures have Marian legionaries in their Macedonian and Punic Wars range.
Miniature Figurines has a Marian legionary in mail in its Late Republican range.
Peter Pig does not have Marian Romans, but their mail-clad Imperial auxiliaries might pass muster.

20mm or 1/72 scale
In 1973 Airfix was the only manufacturer of 20mm plastic miniatures and wargamers exhibited much ingenuity in converting them into troops of other periods and nations. Their Romans – albeit portrayed wearing the legionary equipment of the 1st century AD - and Ancient Britons sets are still in production and could be pressed into service.
See www.plasticsoldierreview.com and you will discover Republican legionaries, cavalry and a wide variety of other figures that might be

used to game Pharsalus.

Wargame Rules suitable for Pharsalus

Conquerors and Kings in Peter Pig's Rules For the Common Man (RFCM) series
De Bellis Magistrorum Militum, Phil Barker, Wargames Research Group, 2010.
Donald Featherstone's Lost Tales, History of Wargaming Project, contains rules for the Ancient period
Field of Glory Rulebook: Ancient and Medieval Wargaming Rules, Richard Bodley Scott, Simon Hall & Terry Shaw, and *Rise of Rome: Field of Glory Republican Rome Army Lists*, Richard Bodley Scott, Osprey Publishing, 2008
The freewargamerules website has numerous sets of rules for Ancient warfare, including the early editions of the Wargames Research Group's Ancient rules.
Junior Generals has both a scenario and simple rules for Pharsalus and Roman paper figures that may be printed off to stage the battle very cheaply
Lost Battles: Reconstructing the Great Clashes of the Ancient World, Philip Sabin, Hambledon Continuum, 2007
Warmaster Ancients, Rick Priestley, Warhammer Historical is more appropriate for a large battle than the *Warhammer Ancient Battles* rules.

Further Reading

Roman Battle Tactics 109BC-AD313, Ross Cowan, Osprey Elite 155, 2007
Roman Legionary 58BC-AD69, Ross Cowan, Osprey Warrior 71, 2003
The Roman Army: the Civil Wars 88-31BC, Nic Field, Osprey Battle Orders 34, 2008
Caesar's Civil War 49-44BC, Adrian Goldsworthy, Osprey Essential Histories 42, 2002
The Complete Roman Army, Adrian Goldsworthy, Thames & Hudson, 2003. See especially pages 181-4.
Pharsalus 48BC: Caesar and Pompey – Clash of the Titans, Simon Sheppard, Osprey Campaign 174, 2006
Warfare in the Classical World, John Warry, Salamander, 1980. See especially pages 171-2.

2. The Battle of Poitiers

19 September 1356

THIS EARLY battle of the Hundred Years War was fought between an English army under the Black Prince and the army of King John of France.

You are Edward, Prince of Wales[13], the leader of the English Army.

Historical Background
The ridge occupied by the English army for about 1,000 yards was thick with scrub and undergrowth, and bounded by a hedge, with its left end falling away to a marsh and its right resting on open ground, strengthened by wagons, earthworks and trenches. Of the two gaps in the hedge, the upper gap was left open, but the lower was barricaded with stakes interlaced with vine branches. Between this ridge and the North Ridge, where the French Army massed, lay cultivated land, partly vines and partly fallow.

Friendly Forces

The English Army, about 6,000 strong, comprised 3,000 men-at-arms, with 2,000 archers and 1,000 sergeants, and was formed into Salisbury's division on the right, Warwick's on the left and the Prince's division, with a small body of mounted men, in reserve in rear. The men-at-arms were deployed into line, and solid wedges of archers were formed up on the flanks of each of the divisions, slightly in advance of them.

Enemy Forces

The French army was about 20,000 strong, including 3,000 crossbowmen and two small contingents of 250 mounted men commanded by Marshals Clermont and Audrehen, and was formed into the Dauphin's division, the Duke of Orleans' division and that of the King. Remembering Crecy, the King of France dismounted his men-at-arms and shortened their lances to a length of about 5 feet.

At a figure-scale of 20 to 1, the English force will consist of 200 dismounted men-at-arms and 100 archers, plus 10 horsemen, and the French 500 men on foot plus 25 cavalry, but the war-game will only require sufficient men-at-arms to form the Dauphin's initial attacking

---

[13] Edward of Woodstock, Prince of Wales, Duke of Cornwall, Prince of Aquitaine (15 June 1330 – 8 June 1376) was the eldest son of Edward III of England and Philippa of Hainault. He is popularly known today as the 'Black Prince', but was not so called in his lifetime.

force of 250 men (representing 5,000) who, when dispersed, can become half the King's force of 500 men (representing 10,000). The Duke of Orleans' column of 5,000 never got into the battle.

Note that the French force should be setup after the English and should be in line with the historical deployment as shown in the historical map at the end of this chapter.

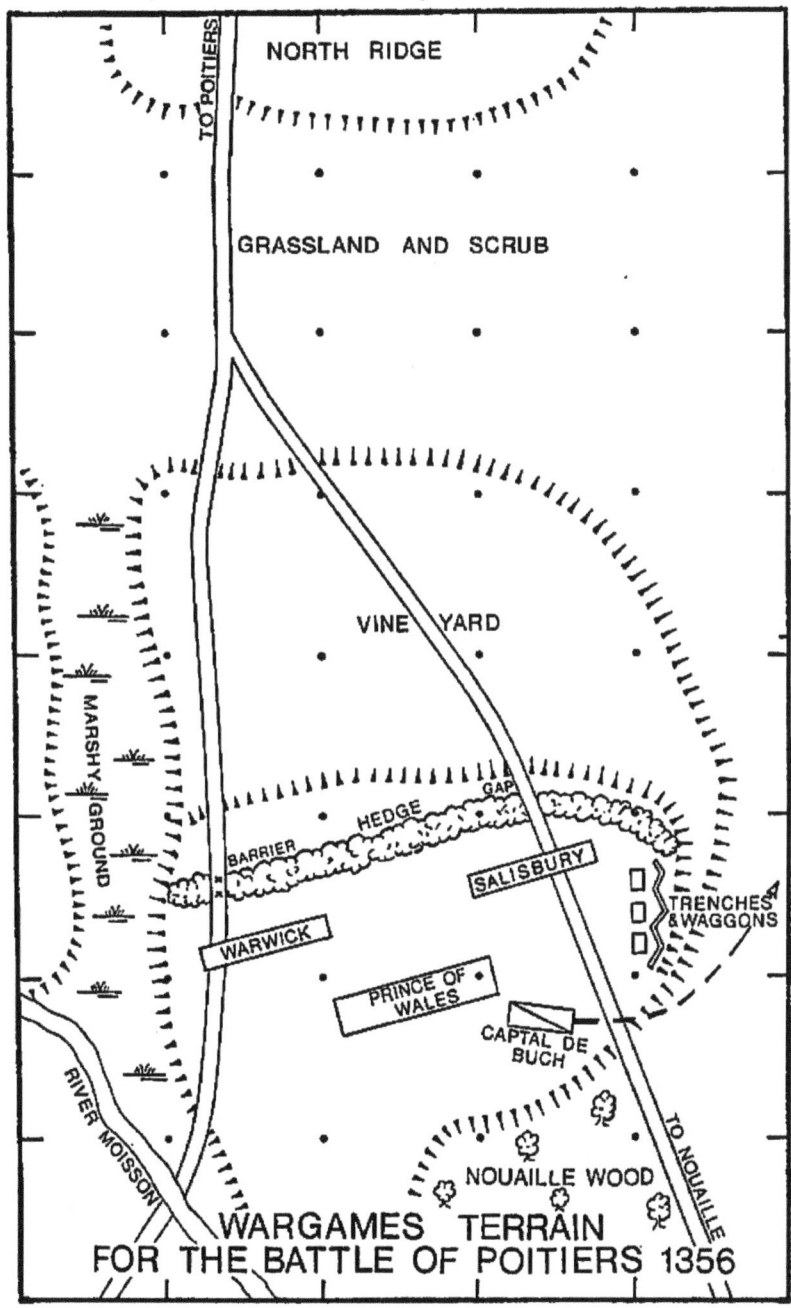

Construction of the terrain

Fight the battle lengthways rather than across the table. The ridge and its approaches cover about 9 square feet, for the first stage of the battle with the horsemen and the Dauphin's column. Extending 4½ feet forward is an area of about 16 square feet for the mêlée with the King's column. This allows sufficient space for the crossbowmen to fire on the mounted English attack on the French King's forces.

The ridge on which the English formed up will cover approximately the lower half of the table, allowing a gradual slope up through the vineyard for the initial cavalry attack and the advance of the Dauphin's column, besides allowing the English archers to get off a reasonable number of shots at the advancing French. This is most important, because it is the firepower of the English archer which really makes possible this battle between two forces of such vastly different strengths.

This terrain may easily be constructed of planks of wood, slabs of polystyrene or books on the table-top, covered first by sheets of newspaper or blankets and then by a green cloth to fall realistically into the right contours. The tracks can either be coloured in or made of strips of suitably coloured adhesive paper. The scrub and vines are simulated by lichen moss.

Stop! Read no further until you have deployed the forces and issued your detailed written orders.

The course of the actual historical battle.

The two French Marshals led their small mounted force forward through the vineyard in a series of small columns, with Clermont's column bunching leftwards on the Nouaille Road while Audrehen followed the Gue de l'Homme track, each path bringing the two columns up against the twin gaps. The English archers on the left of their position kept up a galling fire and caused many casualties. Audrehen's men halted at the manned barricade, which their impatient leader jumped and was captured. Clermont's column passed through the unguarded gap, and swung right to be halted by Salisbury, who moved his line quickly forward, right up to the hedge, so closing the gap and preventing a flank attack on Warwick's division. After severe fighting the cavalry broke and fled; the English soldiers were rigidly restrained from pursuing.

The closely packed ranks of the advancing Dauphin's division were thrown into confusion and disorder as panic-stricken horses crashed through them, but got to grips when the English archers ran out of arrows. The hand-to-hand struggle surged backwards and forwards and, after Warwick's division was reinforced with the Prince's force, the Dauphin's men wavered and drew off in good order.

The division of the young Duke of Orleans was so shaken by the two repulsed attacks that, panic-stricken, it fled in scattered groups from the field. Seeing this, the King's Division of 10,000 men began slowly to advance, rolling forward in a glittering horde that alarmed the weary English. Scornfully dispelling their fears, the Black Prince mounted his force and sent the Gascon the Captal de Buch with 200 cavalry wide out to the right to hit the left flank of the trudging French column.

Led by the Black Prince, the mounted English men-at-arms rolled down the slopes towards the dip that lay between them and the North Ridge, with the mounted archers tacked on to the flanks and rear of their armoured comrades. Seeing the sudden avalanche of men and horses cascading down upon them, the advancing French division stopped, so that the rear ranks piled up on those in front, while others shambled from the field in panic, and before they could assume a defensive formation, the English horsemen crashed into them with a fierce shock that tumbled men and horses to the ground.

In the hard and bloody conflict the outnumbered English forced their way forward yard by yard in a mêlée that surged back and forth. No one saw the Captal de Buch's small body of cavalry coming in from the flank to drive deep into the King's division. The great French column, attacked on two sides, slowly disintegrated as men lurched from the field, until the King of France, realising that all was lost, surrendered. Slowly the battle burned itself out, with the triumphant English pursuing the fleeing French as far as the very walls of Poitiers.

The French casualties were approximately 2,500 killed, some 2,000 captured plus about 4,000 wounded. The English appear to have got off very lightly.

Outline of the enemy's orders.

The battle should commence by two columns of mounted men commanded by Marshals Clermont and Audrehen attacking the hedge barrier at the gap in the hedge and barrier on the road. A roll of 4, 5 or 6 means that the English archers are surprised by the charge from the concealment of the vines and they do not get a volley off before the cavalry charge home.

It is reasonable to consider the possibility that the French would have used the distraction of the cavalry assault to send a flanking column of infantry to attack over the trenches and wagons on the English right. Roll 4, 5 or 6 for this to happen. If it does, roll again 1-2 the column arrives at the obstacles one move before the cavalry attack, 3-4 at the same time, 5-6 one move afterwards.

The main French infantry attack should be subdivided into columns. To reflect the general disorganization, roll 4, 5 or 6 for each column to set off from the French line. Whilst in the area of vines, roll 3, 4, 5 or 6 for each column to move forward through the thick vines. Of course, although delayed, they are largely screened from English archery fire until they emerge in front of the English line.

There is a possibility of the Duke of Orleans could redeploy his battle to cover the flanks for the rest of the French army. Roll 5 or 6 for this to be a possibility.

Ratings of the Commanders and Military Possibilities

In a wargame it is unlikely that the scaled-down force of 25 mounted French men-at-arms who attacked under the two Marshals will be very effective against 300 English in position, plus the massed fire from their archers. To simulate the battle, the cavalry must attack, but Military Possibilities can make their venture more than a suicidal mission. The vineyard can be sufficiently high to mask them from archery fire for most or all of their charge; the height of the vines could produce surprise by the horsemen bursting upon the English (particularly at the point where the gap in the hedge is not barricaded). At that stage the English must check their morale. If the English archers move into the marsh during the charge, their firing time will be taken up.

The Dauphin's column of 5,000 strong (scaled down to 250 dismounted men-at-arms) will attack next—the French *must* attack piecemeal as in 1356—and the trampled vines will cause it to split up into small columns to attack all along the English line. The French must check their state of morale, which will be affected by the retreating cavalry crashing through them plus losses from archery fire. If it is adequate, the English will test their morale to see if they stand— if they flee, the similarity between our reconstruction and the battle itself vanishes with them; but most wargames rules allow a force in position, aided by defensive fire, to repel an attacking force of approximately equal size.

Assuming that the Dauphin's column is repelled as in 1356, there may be a Military Possibility to decide if the English pursue one or both of the defeated French columns and so diminish their numbers. This can be decided by throwing two dice: a total of 4 or less means that both columns are pursued, a total of 5 that the Dauphin's column is pursued, a total of 6 that Orleans' column is pursued, and any total of 7 or over that no pursuit takes place.

If a pursuit is decided on, throw three dice to settle the numbers of pursuers—the combined total being the percentage of the remaining strength of the English force. For example, if the English have 200 men remaining on the table and the dice total is 15, then 15 per cent of their force (30 men) will pursue.

The North Ridge is crowned by the lance pennants of King John's host of 10,000 (scaled down to 500 dismounted men-at-arms). The morale of both French and English must now be considered. Reluctant to attack, the French morale might be low, but the English might suffer a temporary lapse in morale at the thought of attacking such a large force of the enemy. Nothing occurs to raise French morale, whereas English morale quickly rises because of the inspiring personality of the Black Prince. The English dismounted men-at-arms are all replaced by cavalry figures who charge down the hill towards the oncoming dismounted French. The Captal de Buch leads 200 horsemen (scaled down to 10) out in a wide arc to the right, coming in on the French flank, moving off the table (at scaled rates) on to a map of the countryside immediately to the right of the English position, and coming back on the table when they reach the French column. Timing is of primary importance here; de Buch should move *before* the Black Prince. Military Possibility might make them move off simultaneously, besides presenting delaying obstacles to de Buch's progress—a sunken road, a small ravine, thick hedges to hinder his progress or a stretch of marsh that looks like lush green grass. A well designed group of Chance Cards will be very useful at this stage in the battle.

In wargames it has to be decided whether the infantry's morale will allow them to stand against horsemen and, should they stand, whether the cavalry, shaken by their losses from missile fire, suffer in their morale. There were some 3,000 (scaled down to 150) mercenary crossbowmen with the French King's force, and few sets of wargames rules will allow the English to charge home in the face of crossbow fire. It is extremely unlikely in an army of this period, however, that the crossbowmen were deployed in front like skirmishers; they were far more likely to be bunched somewhere in the middle of the column or in the rear. Therefore, probably no more than half of them (possibly far less) will fire upon the oncoming English cavalry. A morale test will reveal whether they hold their ground and fire or let go at long range and flee.

A sprawling hand-to-hand combat will end the battle one way or the other. In 1356 the French were taken unawares by de Buch's flank attack, but that is unlikely in our wargame. A Military Possibility can allow the English commander to send de Buch out to his right or left; the French will then be forced to allocate a force (which will not count in the main mêlée) to watch their flanks. On the other hand, it is possible that Chance Cards, etc, may cause the flanking force to be delayed or never to arrive at all.

Rating of Commanders

The Black Prince must undoubtedly be classified 'above average' as must Warwick and Salisbury and even the Captal de Buch. The French King, the Dauphin and the Duke of Orleans must be classified as 'below average', while one of the two Marshals, Clermont or Audrehen, can be 'above average'.

Notes

These notes – and those to the other chapters – are not exhaustive lists of all the suitable figures, rules and books that are available, and only figures manufactured and/or sold in the United Kingdom are listed. Website, rather than postal, addresses have been given wherever possible.

Wargame Figures suitable for Poitiers

2mm

Irregular Miniatures offer a Medieval Hundred Years' War army in this scale.

6mm or 1/300 scale

Heroics and Ros Wars of the Roses, Crusades and Renaissance ranges may yield suitable figures that can pass muster for Poitiers.

Irregular Miniatures offer Hundred Years' War armies for English and French.

10/12mm

Magister Militum has suitable figures for Poitiers in its Medieval range.

Pendraken Medieval range has many suitable figures

15mm

Essex Miniatures Late Medieval/Early Renaissance range contains suitable figures.

FreiKorp 15 has a Feudal/Medieval range with some 14th century figures.

Irregular Miniatures have many suitable figures in their Medieval range, and also offer ready-made armies for English and French.

Miniature Figurines has Hundred Years' War Crecy period figures.

20mm

When this book was originally published, Airfix was the only manufacturer of soft plastic 20mm toy historical military figures, and made only two sets – Robin Hood and the Sheriff of Nottingham – which contained medieval troops, so early wargamers expended much ingenuity and time in converting them.

Today, the website www.plasticsoldierreview.com/Index.aspx lists several sets for the Hundred Years' War and others for the early medieval period which could also be pressed into service to recreate Poitiers.

Irregular Miniatures have suitable figures in their Late Medieval range.

25/28mm

Essex Miniatures Medieval range has many suitable figures.
Irregular Miniatures have many suitable figures in their Late Feudal and Middle Ages ranges.
Miniature Figurines has a Crecy Period 1300-1350 range.
Old Glory has a Crecy Wars section in its Medieval ranges.

Wargame Rules suitable for Poitiers

Ancient and Medieval Wargaming, Neil Thomas, The History Press
Conquerors and Kings in the Rules For the Common Man (RFCM) series by Peter Pig,
De Bellis Magistrorum Militum, Phil Barker, Wargames Research Group, 2010.
Donald Featherstone's Lost Tales, History of Wargaming Project, contains rules for the Ancient period
Field of Glory Rulebook: Ancient and Medieval Wargaming Rules, Richard Bodley Scott, Simon Hall & Terry Shaw, and *Storm of Arrows* supplement.
The freewargamerules website has numerous sets of rules for Medieval warfare.
The Junior General website has simple rules in a Hundred Years' War – Battle of Agincourt 1415 scenario that could be used to fight Poitiers.
Warmaster Ancients, Rick Priestley, Warhammer Historical is more appropriate for a large battle like Poitiers than the *Warhammer Ancient Battles* rules.

Further Reading
The Armies of Crecy and Poitiers, Christopher Rothero, Osprey Men At Arms 111
The Battle of Poitiers 1356, David Green, The History Press, 2008
The Crecy War: A Military History of the Hundred Years' War from 1337 to the Peace of Bretigny, 1360, Lt.-Col. Alfred H. Burne, Wordsworth, 1999
English Longbowman 1330-1515, Clive Bartlett, Osprey Warrior 11
English Medieval Knight 1300-1400, Christopher Gravett, Osprey Warrior 58
French Armies of the Hundred Years War, David Nicolle, Osprey Men At Arms 337
The Hundred Years' War 1337-1453, Anne Curry, Osprey Essential History 19
Medieval Armies, Terence Wise, Osprey Men At Arms 50
Poitiers 1356: The Capture of a King, David Nicolle, Osprey Campaign 136

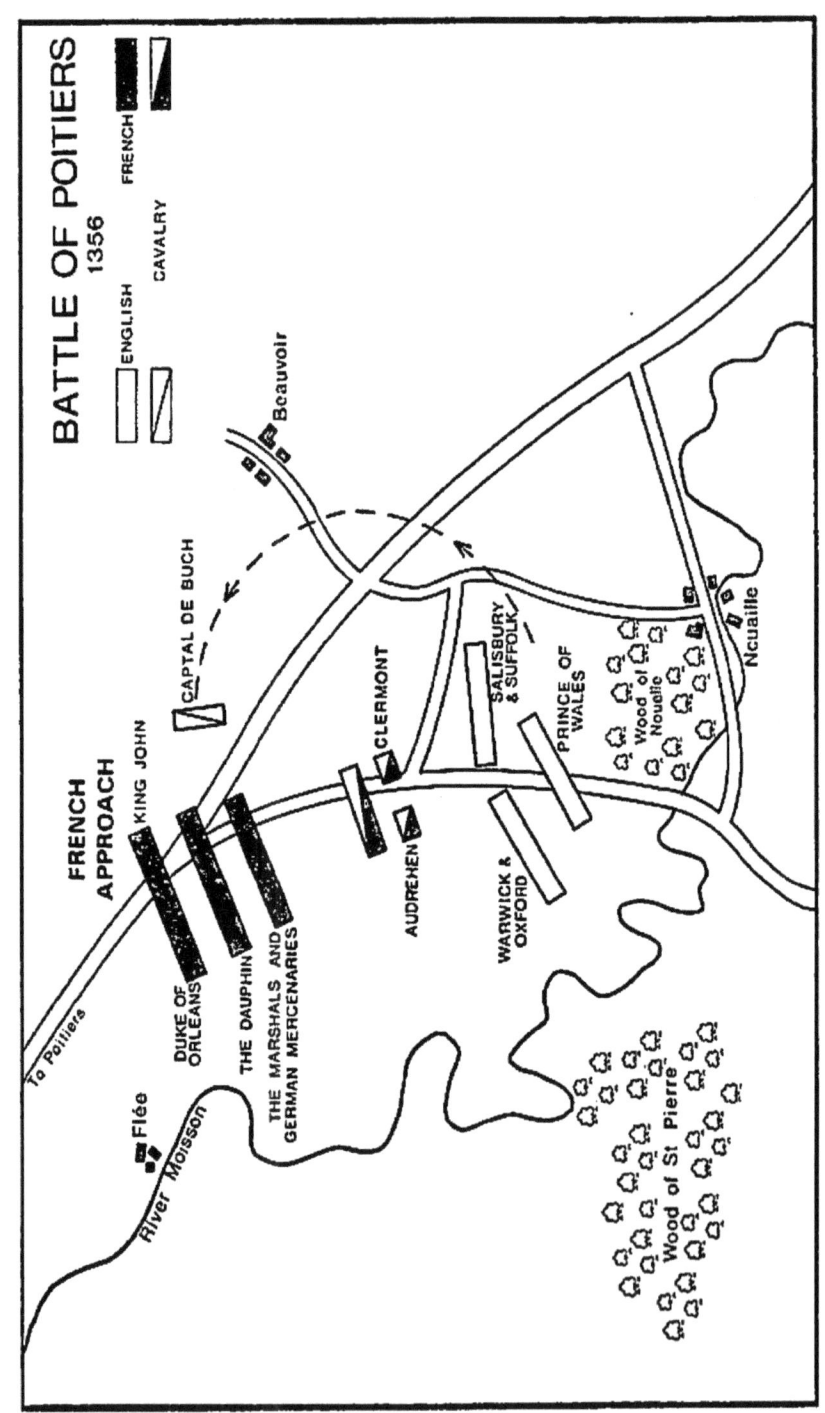

3. The Battle of Barnet

14 April 1471

You are either Edward IV[14] or Richard Neville, Earl of Warwick[15]

Historical Background

THIS BATTLE was fought during the Wars of the Roses between the Yorkists under Edward IV and the Lancastrians under the Earl of Warwick.

Returning from exile in March 1471, Edward IV landed in Yorkshire and marched south. Warwick's opposing forces manoeuvred until the night of Saturday, 13 April, when they positioned themselves near Barnet, the men lying down in their ranks behind a long line of hedges. During the night the Yorkist army reached Barnet, Edward marching them up to Warwick's position in the dark (a rare accomplishment in those days) and drawing them up as best he could. Edward was a good soldier, and realised the necessity of forcing his enemies to fight before they could gather their full strength against him.

Edward drew his troops up in battle order facing Warwick's army on the lower ground beneath the road. In the darkness, Edward's right wing extended beyond Warwick's left, and the latter's right outflanked Edward's left. Realising the enemy were at hand, Warwick opened a fruitless cannonade from his guns posted on his right.

The morning of Easter Sunday, 14 April, brought with it heavy fog, so that the armies groped blindly forward. Edward formed his army up in three bodies, commanding the centre himself, and giving his younger

---

[14] Edward of York (born 28 April 1442), second child of Richard, Duke of York and Cecily Neville, inherited his father's claim to the throne after the latter, together with his younger brother Edmund, was killed at the Battle of Wakefield in 1460. With the support of his cousin, Richard Neville, Earl of Warwick, Edward defeated the Lancastrians in several battles and was proclaimed King Edward IV in London in 1461 whilst Henry VI and his wife, Margaret of Anjou, were campaigning in the north of England. Edward won a decisive victory at Towton, almost wiping out the Lancastrian army. He refused, however, to be Warwick's puppet which caused the latter to join the Lancastrians.

[15] Richard Neville, Earl of Warwick (born 22 November 1428), is now called 'The Kingmaker' because he replaced Henry VI as king of England by his cousin, Edward, Duke of York. Warwick believed he could continue to control the new king. He wanted to arrange a foreign marriage for Edward IV, but in 1464 Edward secretly married Elizabeth Woodville, a commoner. Warwick resented the favours now shown to Elizabeth's relatives and allied himself to Edward's brother George, Duke of Clarence, leading a revolt against the king. Warwick and Clarence then fled to France, where they joined Margaret of Anjou, wife of Henry VI. Margaret's Lancastrian army invaded England in September 1470. Edward fled to the Netherlands until March 1471, when he and his brother Richard, Duke of Gloucester, returned to England.

brother, Richard, Duke of Gloucester, command of the right wing and Lord Hastings command of the left. The Lancastrians were formed up in four groups, with Warwick himself leading the left wing, Exeter on his right, then Montagu, and finally Oxford commanding the right wing.

The Forces

The Lancastrians had 15,000 men and the Yorkists 10,000.

Both armies are known to have had artillery, but Warwick's was the better served. The foot soldiers were equipped with new weapons, for both Edward and Warwick had hired bands of Burgundian hand-gun men. Apart from these professionals, the armies were formed of nobles and their retainers; during the Wars of the Roses the nobles frequently changed their allegiance, so that men were now fighting alongside each other who, in past days, had been bitterly opposed; there were doubt and suspicion of treachery in the air.

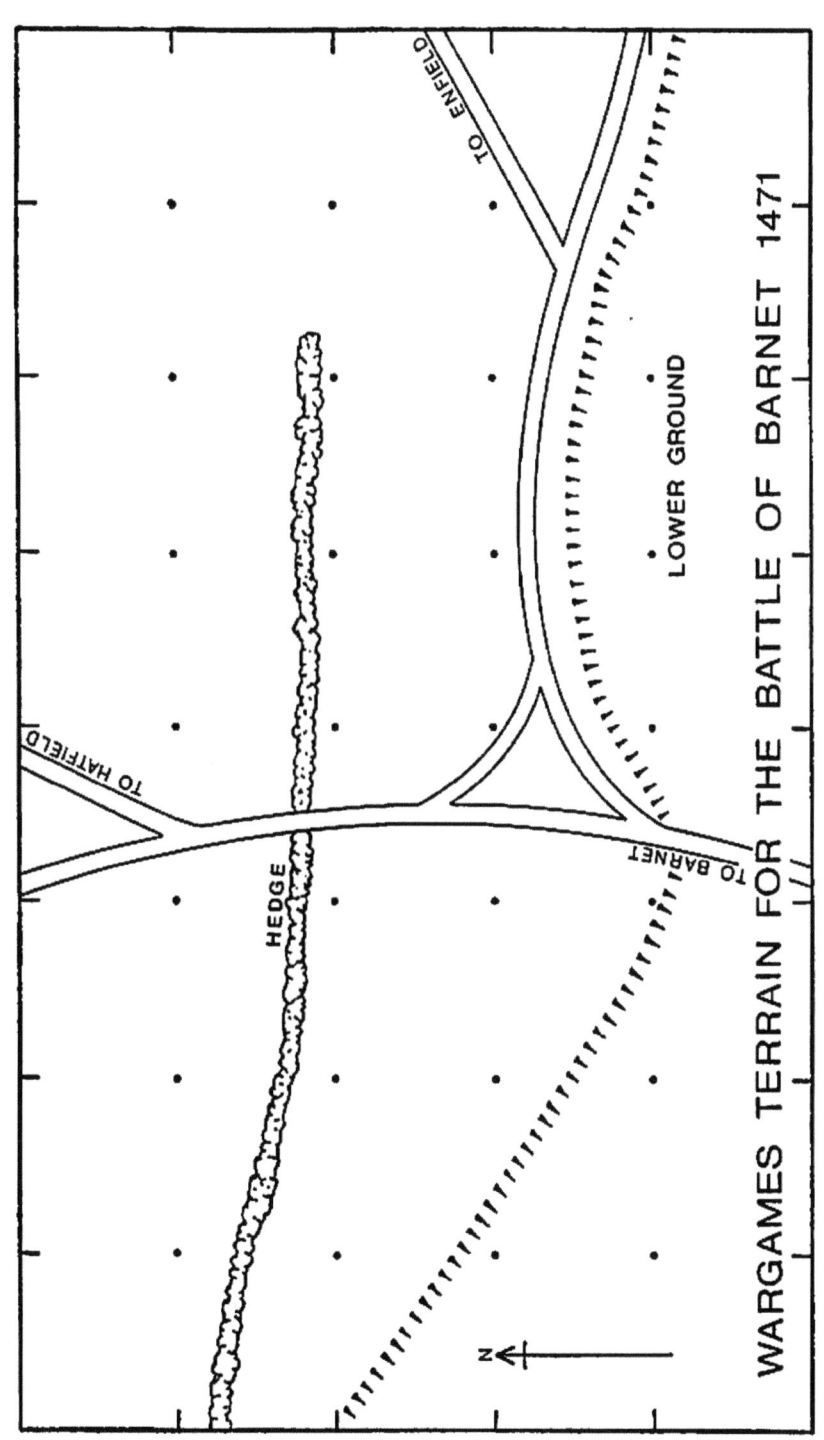

Construction of the terrain

The top three-quarters of the field should form a flat plateau, with the lower or southern part rising up to it (it was here that Edward formed up during the night). Although they play no part in the battle, the tracks shown on historical maps could be included on the table.

Stop! Read no further until you have deployed the forces and issued your detailed written orders.

The course of the actual historical battle.

The battle began in thick fog between 4 and 5 am, with both sides advancing slowly and cautiously, Edward's army having to ascend rising ground. At no time during the day was visibility more than about 20 yd, and as men loomed out of the mist, archers and cannon opened fire. Edward and Montagu were the first to find each other, and rushed in to engage at close quarters. On the Yorkist right Gloucester suddenly came upon Exeter's left flank, which turned and faced him, besides bringing Warwick in on its left, so that Gloucester was engaging both groups. On the Lancastrian right Oxford, an efficient soldier, hit Hastings' left flank, causing his force to break in sudden rout; the broken remnants were chased by cavalry down the road as far as Barnet itself.

Unaware of these events, Warwick could not take advantage of the success of his right wing, so Oxford's pursuit had no effect upon the rest of the battle. Unaware that his left was in the air, Edward continued pressing Montagu hard and getting the better of his West Country bowmen and billmen. Exeter, with his men well in hand, appears to have given some assistance to Montagu's hard-pressed force. Montagu had told his men to keep in line with Exeter's, who, to meet Gloucester's attack had turned to face eastwards; both armies had gradually turned anticlockwise until they were at 90° to their starting positions.

Oxford halted and reformed his men, to return to where the Yorkists should have been, and came upon the exposed flank of a large body of men looming out of the mist. This force, which was actually Montagu's Lancastrians, mistook Oxford's De Vere badge of a star for Edward's sun device, and loosed volleys of arrows as Oxford's men charged into them. Suddenly recognising each other, both sides raised the cry of treason, always common in the Wars of the Roses, and many fled towards the Yorkists, who simply cut them down. There was general confusion.

Oxford, convinced that he had been betrayed, left the field. The cry of treason passed from man to man down the already hard-pressed centre of the Lancastrian army; Montagu and his men found themselves under attack from two sides and Montagu himself was killed. Pushing steadily forward, Edward then fell on Exeter, who fled the field followed by his men. Only Warwick's wing was left to maintain the combat, but, seeing that all was lost, he left the field, to be speedily overtaken and slain. Edward ordered 'no quarter', and estimates of the Lancastrian dead range from 4,000 to 10,000.

This battle could be reconstructed as three separate actions, perhaps in different rooms: (1) the battle between Edward and Montagu, (2) Gloucester against Exeter and Warwick, and (3) Oxford's rout of Hastings. The division into three actions simulates the confusion caused by the fog. When Oxford's returning troops blunder into Montagu's flank, all six war-gamers could join together on one large table to finish off the battle.

Outline of the enemy's orders.

To recreate the problems of command and control caused by the dense fog cards can be used. Each unit should be dealt a card from just one suit from a pack of cards. The units moving in the order of the cards with the lowest card moving first (ace being low).

As each unit is about to move the wargamer should state two options, for example 'advance' or 'halt'. For each enemy unit, the a simple die roll should decide which action the unit takes (1, 2, or 3 it takes the first option, 4, 5 or 6 it takes the second option). For each friendly unit, roll 1 or 2 it takes the first option, 3 or 4 the second option, 5 or 6 the player may decide the appropriate action. This should generate some of the chaos of the original battle, without completely removing all control from the wargamer.

Ratings of the Commanders and Military Possibilities

Edward should be classified as 'above average'; Fortescue writes that, despite the manner in which the fog became his ally, victory was due to Edward's promptness and his rapidity of decision, which stamped him as a soldier far in advance of his time. Warwick, who was also a very fine soldier, did not show up at his best in this battle—he should be classed as 'average', together with Montagu, Exeter and Gloucester. Oxford could be classified as 'above average', since his rout of Hastings was a well conducted affair. He might be credited with extra morale power to rally his soldiers and bring them back to the battle, since his return is a vital aspect of the Battle of Barnet.

The element of surprise here will be far from easy to simulate, and it is suggested that all formations move on the map, using tracings. Only when two forces moving on the map appear within a charge-move distance of each other should they be placed on the wargames table.

Edward's night march before the battle, including his final deployment, could be marked on a map, so that uncertainty will creep into the positioning of his forces. This may preclude Oxford from outflanking Hastings, and Gloucester from pinning down both Warwick and Exeter. Military Possibilities have to be considered in these cases.

The shaky loyalties of the troops at Barnet should be exemplified in the morale rules, which should be formulated to allow formations to break and rally easily; they may return to the fray somewhat timidly.

Simulating the difficulties of fighting in a fog can be handled by an 'Obscurity Factor', using 'mild' Chance Cards bearing relatively marginal instructions such as 'Unit (formation) moves 3 inches forward ... or back ... or half left or right... or back-wards', each alternative being marked on a separate card. There are innumerable minor manoeuvres that will simulate the uncertainty of men moving in the face of an unseen enemy.

Oxford's rout of Hastings abounds with Military Possibilities. For the sake of realism, Hastings must be initially chased off, otherwise Oxford will not be able to return and create the confusion that led to the Lancastrian defeat. Some local rule must ensure that Hastings is hit in the flank and goes—perhaps Oxford's force could be made stronger than that of Hastings. Another Military Possibility could be to allow Hastings to make a semi-fighting withdrawal, delaying Oxford's return to the field. Anyhow, it has to be decided how far Oxford's men chase and how long it takes him to get them under control—this is largely a question of their morale. Military Possibilities could delay that regrouping so that the three forces of Warwick, Exeter and Montagu might have the time to defeat those of Edward and Gloucester.

Another vital aspect of the battle was the manner in which the forces wheeled, causing Oxford's men on their return to hit Montagu in flank. This can be worked by assuming that Edward and Montagu (who made the first contact) edged forward towards each other to meet on or south of the crossroads. As Gloucester was able to hold the combined forces of Exeter and Warwick, it is reasonable to assume that initially he might force Exeter back and, as Warwick moves forward, both end up facing east, presenting a united force against Gloucester.

Montagu's archers fired upon Oxford's men as they loomed up out of the mist, but there is no mist over our table-top battlefield nor will any wargamer fire upon his own men. By giving Montagu's archers some uncontrolled reaction (as described in the Ancient and Mediaeval Rules of the Wargames Research Group), one could force them to fire, or the matter could be handled by judiciously worded Chance Cards.

If neither wargamer is informed that it is the Battle of Barnet he is fighting, the wargamer representing Montagu may be told that a force is coming up fast on his flank (on the map) and will be on the table during the next move, coming within bow range of his ranks. He can then be given the options of holding his fire to see if they are friends or firing as soon as they appear. Oxford's men, coming on to the table from the map, may also be informed that they will be arriving on the flank of a force at the same time as they are placed in position on the table, and that this force may fire upon them.

Rules must be formulated to cover the firing of artillery and handguns, and to represent their undoubted effect upon morale. To cover the deaths of Warwick and Montagu, it is suggested that 'single combat' be built into the game, detailed instructions for which are given in *Advanced Wargames*.

Notes

These notes – and those to the other chapters – are not exhaustive lists of all the suitable figures, rules and books that are available, and only figures manufactured and/or sold in the United Kingdom are listed. Website, rather than postal, addresses have been given wherever possible.

Wargame Figures suitable for Barnet
2mm

Irregular Miniatures offer ready-made Wars of the Roses armies.

6mm or 1/300 scale

Baccus6mm has a Wars of the Roses range and also sells flags and banners.

Heroics and Ros have a Wars of the Roses 1455-1485 range, and other suitable figures in their small Italian Wars Renaissance range.

Irregular Miniatures offer ready-made armies for the Wars of the Roses.

10/12mm

Magister Militum has Medieval figures suitable for Barnet.

Old Glory UK Grand Scale has a High Medieval and Early Renaissance range which contains suitable figures.

Pendraken Late Medieval range has figures for the Wars of the Roses,

15mm

Essex Miniatures Late Medieval/Early Renaissance range has suitable figures.

FreiKorp 15 has a Wars of the Roses 1455-1487 range.

Irregular Miniatures Medieval (1100-1500) range has suitable figures.

Miniature Figurines has a Wars of the Roses range.

Peter Pig has a Wars of the Roses range.

20mm

When this book was originally published, Airfix was the only manufacturer of soft plastic 20mm toy historical military figures, and made only two sets – Robin Hood and the Sheriff of Nottingham – which contained medieval troops, so early wargamers expended much ingenuity and time in converting them.

Today, the website www.plasticsoldierreview.com/Index.aspx lists several sets for the Hundred Years' War and early medieval period which could be pressed into service to recreate Barnet.

Irregular Miniatures have suitable figures in their Late Medieval range.

25/28mm

Essex Miniatures Later Medieval range has suitable dismounted knights and other figures.

Irregular Miniatures have suitable figures in their Middle Ages (1400-1500) range.

Miniature Figurines has a Wars of the Roses range which includes figures of Edward IV and the Earl of Warwick.

Old Glory has a Wars of the Roses range.

Perry Miniatures has an Agincourt to Orleans range with many suitable metal figures, and has plastic Wars of the Roses infantry and command sets.

Wargame Rules suitable for Barnet

A Crown of Paper campaign game for the Wars of the Roses, The Perfect Captain
Ancient & Medieval Wargaming, Neil Thomas,
Bloody Barons: The Wars of the Roses, Peter Pig Rules For the Common Man (RFCM), Peter Pig
De Bellis Magistrorum Militum, Phil Barker, Wargames Research Group, 2010.
Donald Featherstone's Lost Tales, History of Wargaming Project, contains rules for the Medieval period
Field of Glory Rulebook: Ancient and Medieval Wargaming Rules, Richard Bodley Scott, Simon Hall & Terry Shaw, and *Storm of Arrows* supplement
For, Lords, Tomorrow is a Busy Day – A War of the Roses complete battlefield rules and mini-campaign system, Realistic Modelling Services
The freewargamerules website has numerous sets of rules for Medieval warfare.
The Junior General website has simple rules in a War of the Roses – Battle of Towton 1461 scenario that could be used to fight Barnet.
Warmaster Ancients, Rick Priestley, Warhammer Historical is more appropriate for a large battle such as Barnet than the *Warhammer*

Ancient Battles rules.

Further Reading

Barnet – 1471: Death of the Kingmaker, David Clark, Battleground Wars of the Roses, Pen & Sword, 2006
The Battlefields of England, Alfred H. Burne, Penguin Classic Military History, 1996
The Battles of Barnet and Tewkesbury, P. W. Hammond, Palgrave Macmillan, 1993
Cassell's Battlefields of Britain & Ireland, Richard Brooks, Weidenfield & Nicolson, (2005).
English Longbowman 1330-1515, Clive Bartlett, Osprey Warrior 11
English Medieval Knight 1400-1500, Christopher Gravett, Osprey Warrior 35
Medieval Handgonnes: The first black powder infantry weapons, Sean McLachlan, Osprey Weapon 3
Tewkesbury1471: The last Yorkist victory, Christopher Gravett, Osprey Campaign 131 also contains a detailed account of Barnet
The Wars of the Roses 1455-1485, Michael Hicks, Osprey Essential History 54
The Wars of the Roses, Terence Wise, Osprey Men At Arms 145
Warwick The Kingmaker, Paul Murray Kendall, Phoenix Press, 2003

The historical battlefield map

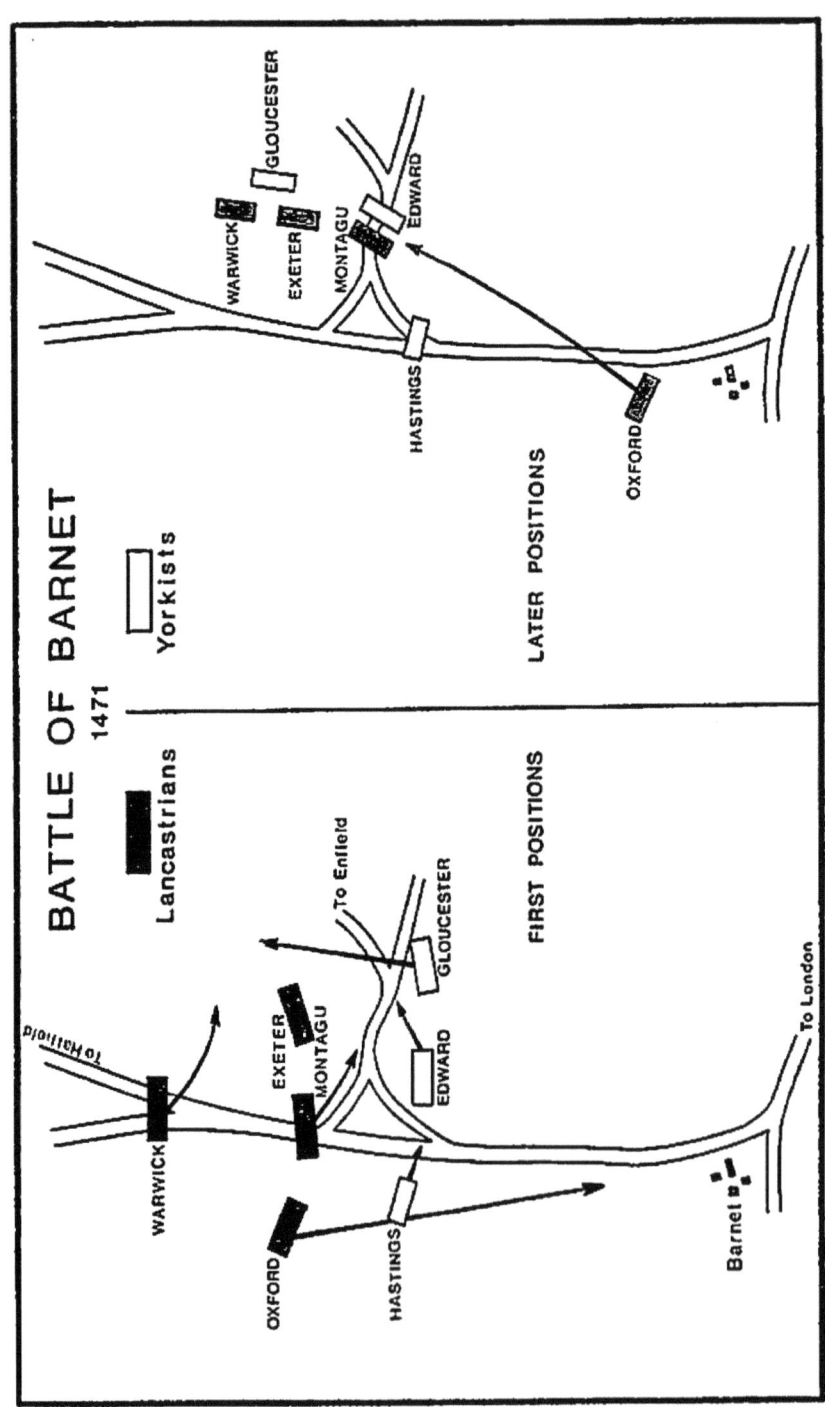

46

4. The Battle of Cheriton

29 March 1644

You are General Sir William Waller[16] of the Parliamentarian Army.

Historical Background

THIS BATTLE was fought during the English Civil War between a Royalist army under Lord Hopton and a Parliamentary force commanded by General Sir William Waller.

On 28 March 1644 the Royalist army camped on a horseshoe-shaped ridge, their guns placed to cover Cheriton Wood on their left. Forward in a little wood on a parallel ridge to the south was a detachment of 1,000 musketeers and 500 horse under Sir George Lisle. Next morning, two hours after sunrise, when the thick mist lifted, masses of Roundhead cavalry were seen deploying on the southern slopes of the ridge where Lisle was posted. Dangerously exposed, his force, covered by cavalry, had to retire. Parliamentary forces then moved forward and occupied Lisle's former position. Waller sent a force of cavalry down into the valley in front of his guns and 9 regiments of infantry, each drawn up six deep, with 5 regiments forward and 4 behind, lined the ridge behind hedgerows from Cheriton Wood towards the village of Cheriton.

---

[16] William Waller (born c1598) became MP for Andover in 1640. A strict Presbyterian and a member of the opposition to Charles I, he became a prominent Parliamentarian when the Civil War broke out in 1642. He received an appointment as a colonel, and successfully concluded the siege of Portsmouth in September 1642; later the same year he captured Farnham and Winchester. In 1643 Waller was promoted to major-general and placed in charge of operations in the Gloucester –Bristol region. He won a victory at Higham and captured Hereford.

He then opposed the advance of Sir Ralph Hopton – a personal friend - and the Royalist western army, and though defeated in the Battle of Lansdown he was able to encircle Hopton in Devizes. However, Hopton and a relieving force from Oxford inflicted a crushing defeat upon Waller's army at the Battle of Roundway Down on 13 July 1643.

Waller'ss new forces were local troops, who resented long marches and hard work far from their own counties, and were liable to. Mutiny, desert and even march home in formed bodies under their officers. Their bravery at the surprise of Alton, the skirmish at the St Lawrence's church in December 1643 and the recapture of Arundel in January 1644, only partially redeemed their generally bad conduct.

Waller was a skilful general, described as 'the best shifter and chooser of ground' on either side, at his best at the head of a small and highly-disciplined regular army.

Royalist Forces The Royalist army consists of 3,500 infantry, 2,500 cavalry and 10 guns. However, due to the mist, their initial defensive dispositions are unclear.

Parlimentarian Forces The Parliamentary Army consisted of 6,000 infantry, 4,000 cavalry and 15 guns; the infantry included White and Yellow Regiments of the London Brigade and Horse and Foot from Kent, and the large cavalry force under Sir William Balfour included Hazelrig's cuirassiers, known as the 'Lobsters' because of their iron armour. A useful addition was Colonel Norton and his troop of Hambledon Boys, who knew the countryside around Cheriton.

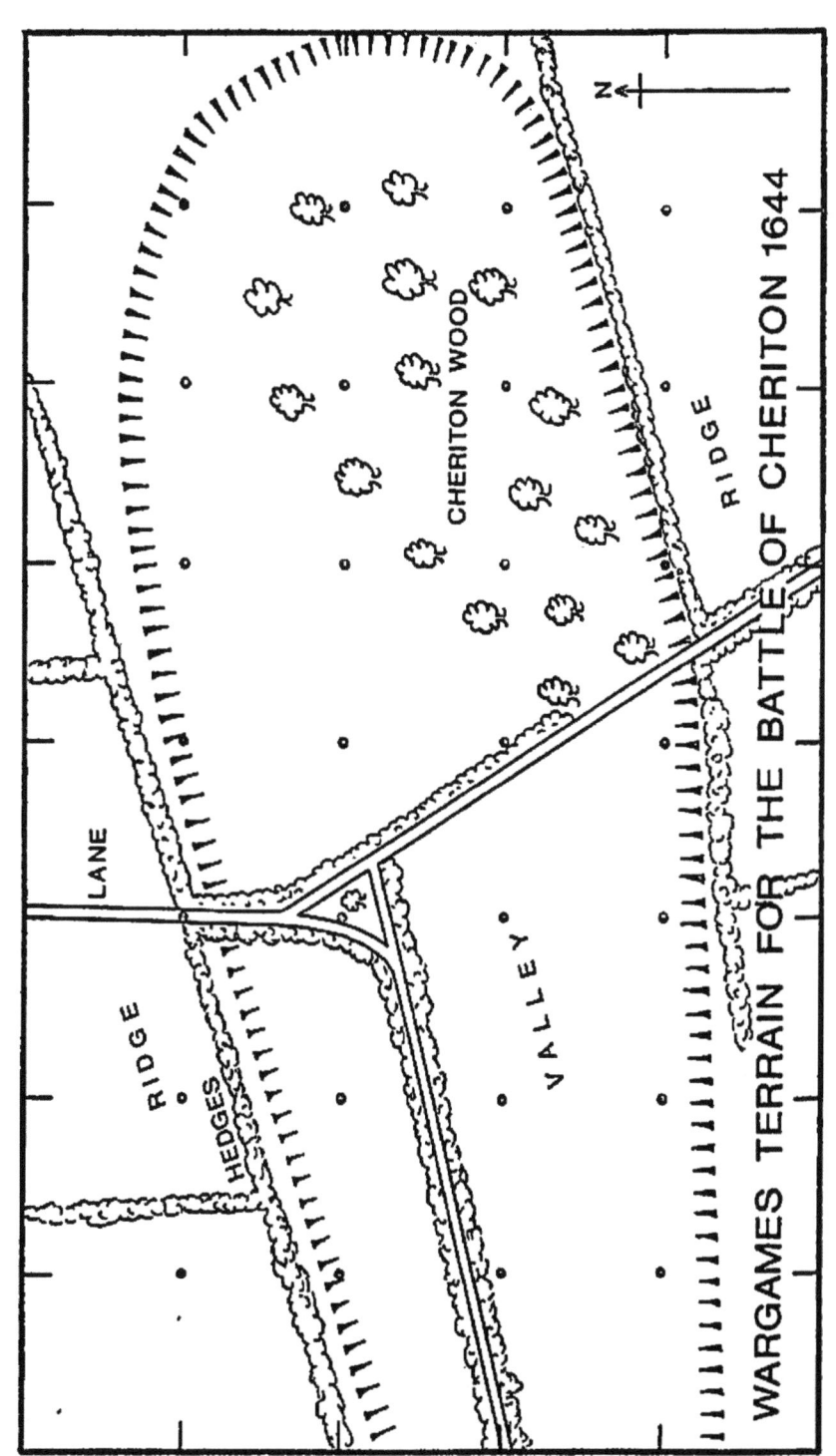

Construction of the terrain

The bulk of the action took place in and around Cheriton Wood and in the valley to the left of the lane that bisects the terrain. Both armies were positioned behind hedges on rising ground at the north and south ends of the table. The entire north and south quarters of the table need to be raised by slabs of polystyrene, planks, or any other means, to a height of about 4 inches and then covered with a cloth depressed to form the valley that runs across the middle of the table. Cheriton Wood need not be as dense as shown on the map, but can be a sheet of green-painted hardboard with a few symbolic trees dotted around its edges. The hedges play an essential part not only because they deterred attack when lined with musketeers and pikemen but because hedges bordered the narrow lane and channelled the Royalist cavalry, squadron by squadron, down into the valley below.

Stop! Read no further until you have deployed the forces and issued your detailed written orders.

The course of the actual historical battle

About 1,000 men of the London Brigade went forward to capture Cheriton Wood, where hand-to-hand fighting took place with Sir George Lisle's men. Hopton had foreseen this attack and planted some drakes (field-pieces) on the high ground north-east of the wood; when the London Brigade surged out from the trees, they ran into the point-blank fire of these guns, which forced them to retreat to the shelter of the wood. Royalist musketeers who followed them were repulsed, but Royalist infantry outflanked the Roundheads on the east of the wood and threw the London Brigade back in disorder. The Royalists then reoccupied the wood.

Waller had posted his Horse in such a position that if the Royalist cavalry approached they had to come down a lane and could only deploy one regiment at a time. But Hopton, in such a strong position that it was best to stand fast and make Waller decide whether to attack him or withdraw from the field, did not intend to take any cavalry action.

However, Sir Henry Bard, a young and impetuous cavalry commander, could not resist attacking the Roundhead cavalry whom he saw drawn up in front of him. His regiment charged down the lane towards them, taking fire from musketeers posted behind hedges and in coppices. Bard was killed and his horsemen overwhelmed, but troop after troop of Royalist cavalry poured down the lane after him, to be defeated in detail by the Parliamentary horse and musketeers as they emerged on to the open ground. Before long all the Royalist cavalry on the right had been defeated and Hopton's flank was open to attack; so, to retrieve the situation, the infantry were sent down and, meeting the

Parliamentary foot soldiers, they came to 'push of pike' with both sides fighting stoutly. Eventually Hazelrig's Lobsters swept round behind the Royalist cavalry and into the infantry, driving them back in disorder. Before that, a force of Parliamentary musketeers came out from their cover and fell upon the flank of the Royalist cavalry so putting the final touch to their discomfiture.

Another Parliamentary infantry attack on Cheriton Woods drove out the Royalist infantry, so that the whole Royalist line fell back on its original position while the last of Hopton's cavalry sealed off the end of the lane. The Royalist force withdrew during the night to Basing. Casualties were 900 killed and wounded in the Parliamentary army and 1,400 in the Royalist.

Outline of the enemy's orders.

Commanded by Lords Hopton on the left and Forth on the right, the Royalist army of 3,500 infantry, 2,500 cavalry and 10 guns, was formed up with infantry in the centre and cavalry on wings. Facing Cheriton Wood, Hopton's infantry were drawn up on reverse slopes. The Royalist army included the Queen's Regiment of cavalry, which had many Frenchmen in its ranks, and some redcoated Irish infantry regiments.

The artillery should be concentrated to protect Cheriton Wood, on the high ground north-east of the wood.

If Cheriton Wood is taken, then the Royalist army should attempt a counter-attack.

Roll a die for the Royalist cavalry: 1, 2, 3 or 4 they attack by single regiments down the main track in the middle of the battleground.

Ratings of the Commanders and Military Possibilities

Forth, Hopton, Waller and Balfour are 'average'; Bard and Lisle 'below average'.

The initial deployment of both forces in the mist can be simulated by moving them on maps, bringing them to the table when it is considered that the mist has lifted and they can see each other. Lisle's withdrawal during the opening stage of the battle could be subject to a Military Possibility, so that he fights instead of withdrawing, although the degree to which this is carried out could materially affect the later accuracy of the reconstruction. Hopton's infantry, drawn up on the reverse slopes facing Cheriton Wood, were not visible to the Parliamentarians—this could be simulated by marking them on the map but not placing them on the table.

About 1,000 musketeers of the London Brigade chased the same number of Royalist musketeers out of Cheriton Wood; this will be an even struggle on the wargames table and, without the aid of any Military Possibility, the Royalists might well throw back the London Brigade. To retain realism, therefore, the latter could be given a bonus in both morale and fighting ability, so as to ensure that they follow the historical precedent of capturing the wood. When the London Brigade emerged from the wood they ran into point-blank artillery fire, which caused their morale to falter; in 1644 they recoiled, and since it is desirable that they do so in the reconstruction, 'local' rules might be required. (On the other hand, Military Possibility might prevent the London Brigade from being beaten back, so that they attack the guns, perhaps capturing them.) The morale of the Parliamentary musketeers must rise when back in the shelter of the trees, because again they defeat their Royalist pursuers; but then more Royalists outflank them east of the wood and drive them out in disorder. A Military Possibility might enable the London Brigade to stand, so that throughout the course of the battle Cheriton Wood is held by Parliament.

At this stage Hopton, with his smaller army, wished to stand on the defensive and await Waller's attack; a Military Possibility might prevent Bard from charging down the lane at the head of his cavalry and precipitating the defeat of the Royalist horsemen at the hands of Parliamentary cavalry. But this is inaccurate and Military Possibility should be heavily weighed so that Bard *does* go. However, if he does not charge, Waller will either have to come forward and attack Hopton or withdraw from the field, leaving it in the possession of the Royalists. A Military Possibility could determine whether the rest of the cavalry follow Bard, how many of them do so, whether they go down at such intervals as to support each other or whether the massed Parliamentary cavalry at the foot of the lane is given sufficient time to destroy each squadron as it emerges. This might be the place for some sort of uncontrolled attack (as provided for in the Wargames Research Group's Ancient Rules). Another Military Possibility could allow the Royalist cavalry to hold their own or even be victorious—but this is so historically unrealistic as to destroy any semblance of a true reconstruction of the battle.

In the 'push of pike' that followed the Royalists held their own until Parliamentary cavalry burst through the Royalist horsemen and got round in their rear. Military Possibilities here could include a Royalist victory in the infantry battle or some factor preventing the Parliamentary cavalry from getting round behind the Royalist foot. Both these Military Possibilities are feasible in a battle that was never a runaway victory for Parliament. However, if the reconstruction follows history, the battle finishes with a Parliamentary infantry attack on Cheriton Wood, forcing the Royalists to fall back to their original position, with the remnants of Hopton's cavalry sealing off the end of the lane. This allows an opportunity for an interesting rearguard action, without any Military Possibilities.

Notes

These notes – and those to the other chapters – are not exhaustive lists of all the suitable figures, rules and books that are available, and only figures manufactured and/or sold in the United Kingdom are listed. Website, rather than postal, addresses have been given wherever possible.

Wargame Figures suitable for Cheriton
2mm

Irregular Miniatures have a Renaissance range containing figures suitable for the English Civil Wars

6mm or 1/300 scale

Baccus has an extensive English Civil War range. The website also has information on uniforms and colours.

Heroics and Ros has a range for the English Civil Wars.

Irregular Miniatures have a Late Renaissance range suitable for the English Civil Wars.

10/12mm

Miniature Figurines, now owned by Caliver Books of Nottingham has a 12mm English Civil War range.

Old Glory UK Grand Scale has an English Civil War range.

Pendraken has an English Civil Wars ranges.

15mm

Essex Miniatures has a Renaissance range containing soldiers of the English Civil Wars.

FreiKorp 15 has an English Civil War 1642-51 range and an ECW and 30 Years' War 1618-48 range with suitable troops.

Irregular Miniatures have a Renaissance 1600-1700 range suitable for the English Civil Wars.

Matchlock Miniatures, owned by Caliver Books of Nottingham, has a Pike & Shot range covering the English Civil Wars, which includes characters such as Puritan preachers, witchfinders and a wounded man being treated by a surgeon.

Miniature Figurines has figures suitable for the English Civil Wars.

Peter Pig has an English Civil War range.

20mm

The website www.plasticsoldierreview.com/Index.aspx lists only four sets for the English Civil War, but there are others in the Thirty Years' War listing which could also be used to recreate Cheriton.

25/28mm

Essex Miniatures has a Renaissance range containing the English Civil Wars.

Foundry Miniatures have an extensive English Civil Wars range.

Irregular Miniatures Renaissance range contains English Civil wars figures.

Matchlock Miniatures, owned by Caliver Books of Nottingham has a Pike & Shot range which covers the English Civil Wars.

Miniature Figurines has a range for the English Civil Wars.

Old Glory has ranges for the English Civil Wars.

Perry Miniatures has a range of metal figures for the English Civil Wars.

Warlord Games has a growing Pike & Shotte range of metal and hard plastic figures for the English Civil Wars.

Wargame Rules suitable for Cheriton
1644: Rules for Battles of the English Civil War, Rick Priestley, Foundry Publications

Field of Glory Renaissance, Richard Bodley Scott, Osprey/Slitherine,

The freewargamerules website has several sets of rules for the English Civil Wars in the Renaissance section.

Impetus: game rules for miniature battles [tactical rules for Ancient, Medieval and Renaissance periods], Dadi & Piombo; the free to download *Basic Baroque* expansion has rules and army lists for the English Civil Wars.

The Junior General website has simple rules in scenarios for Marston Moor and Naseby that could be used to fight Cheriton, and paper figures for the period.

Pike and Shot English Civil War Wargame Rules, John Armatys, free to download at:
    www.wargamedevelopments.org/game_downloads/Pands.pdf

Polemos English Civil War [tactical rules for larger battles], Peter Berry, may be purchased as hard copy or pdf from:

Regiment of Foote [ECW tactical], Peter Pig Rules For the Common Man

Tinker Fox [ECW campaign system], The Perfect Captain website:

Very Civile Actions [ECW tactical rules], The Perfect Captain website

Wargames Campaigns [campaign and simple tactical rules in ECW Battle of Alton Church scenario], D. F. Featherstone (1970)

Wargames Through the Ages, Vol. II, *1420-1783,* D. F. Featherstone (1974)

Wargaming: An Introduction [contains simple Pike and Shot period rules], Neil Thomas, The History Press Ltd

Wargaming Pike and Shot, Charlie Wesencraft, History of Wargaming Project

Warhammer English Civil War, John Stallard, Warhammer Historical

Further Reading
The Battlefields of England, Alfred H. Burne, Penguin Classic Military History, 1996
The Battle of Cheriton 1644, Lawrence Spring, Stuart Press, 1997
Cassell's Battlefields of Britain & Ireland, Richard Brooks, Weidenfield & Nicolson, (2005).
Cheriton 1644: The Campaign and the Battle, John Adair, Kineton, 1973
Decisive Battles of the English Civil War, Malcolm Wanklyn, Pen and Sword
Going to the Wars: The Experience of the English Civil Wars, 1638-1651, Charles Carleton, Routledge, 1992
A Military History of the English Civil War: 1642-1649, Malcolm Wanklyn and Frank Jones, Longman
Roundhead General: The Campaigns of Sir William Waller, John Adair, Sutton Publishing, 1997
Soldiers of the English Civil War 1: Infantry, Keith Roberts, Osprey Elite 25
Soldiers of the English Civil War 2: Cavalry, John Tincey, Osprey Elite 27
The English Civil Wars 1642-51, Peter Gaunt, Osprey Essential History 58
The English Civil War 1642-1651: An Illustrated Military History, Philip Haythornthwaite, Blandford Press Ltd.
English Civil War Artillery 1642-51, Chris Henry, Osprey New Vanguard 108
Ironsides: English Cavalry 1588-1688, John Tincey, Osprey Warrior

The historical battlefield map

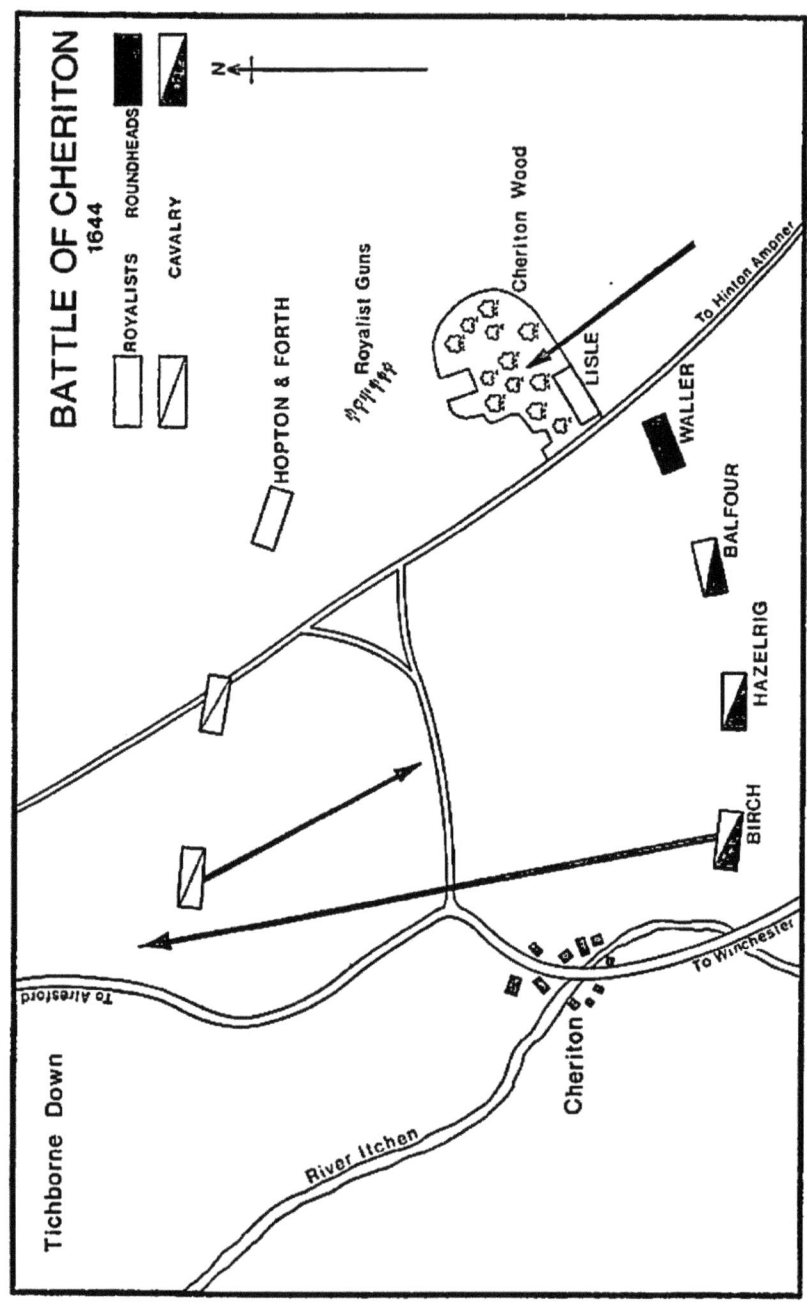

5. The Battle of Wynendael

28 September 1708

You are General Webb[17], commanding the forces protecting the convoy against a superior French force.

Historical Background

THIS LITTLE known but typical small conflict, which took place during Marlborough's campaign in the Low Countries, is ideal for reconstruction. On 27 September 1708 a convoy of 700 wagons, escorted by 12 battalions of infantry, set out from Ostend for Lille, which Marlborough was besieging. To supply further protection to the convoy, General Webb marched with another 12 battalions to Thourout, while Cadogan took 26 squadrons of cavalry to Roulers, two towns on the convoy's route. Vendome, the French Commander, had sent Count de la Mothe at the head of a substantial force to intercept the convoy.

On the following morning Count Lottum, sent with 150 horse by Cadogan to meet the convoy, reported that he had struck a strong French force at Ichtegem, two miles beyond Wynendael and four miles from Thourout on the Ostend road. Webb collected all his available infantry battalions and set off, with Lottum's squadron patrolling ahead, and, emerging from a wood-bordered defile on to a heathy plain, his cavalry came upon de la Mothe's advancing columns. The cavalry skirmished as they slowly retired, giving Webb time to form his men into two lines across the entrance to the defile, battalion by battalion as they marched up, his right resting on the Castle of Wynendael. Prussian and Dutch infantry together with Grenadiers were posted in the woods on either side.

Friendly Forces Webb's force, totalling 6,000 men, was formed of Dutch, Prussian and Hanoverian troops, including Orkeney's Royal Scots, Preston's Cameronians, and Collyer's and Murray's Scots-Dutch. He had no artillery.

---

[17] General John Richmond Webb (born 26 December 1667) was as commissioned as a Cornet of Dragoons in 1687. He entered Parliament in 1695 as Tory member and became a close political follower of St John. In the same year, he was promoted to Colonel of Princess Anne of Denmark's Regiment of Foot. He served in Flanders in the campaign of 1702-1703, was a Brigadier at the Battle of Blenheim in 1704 and a Major-General at Ramillies and Oudenarde.

Enemy Forces The French force consisted of about 24,000 men, made up of 60 squadrons of cavalry, 34 battalions of infantry and at least 20 guns.

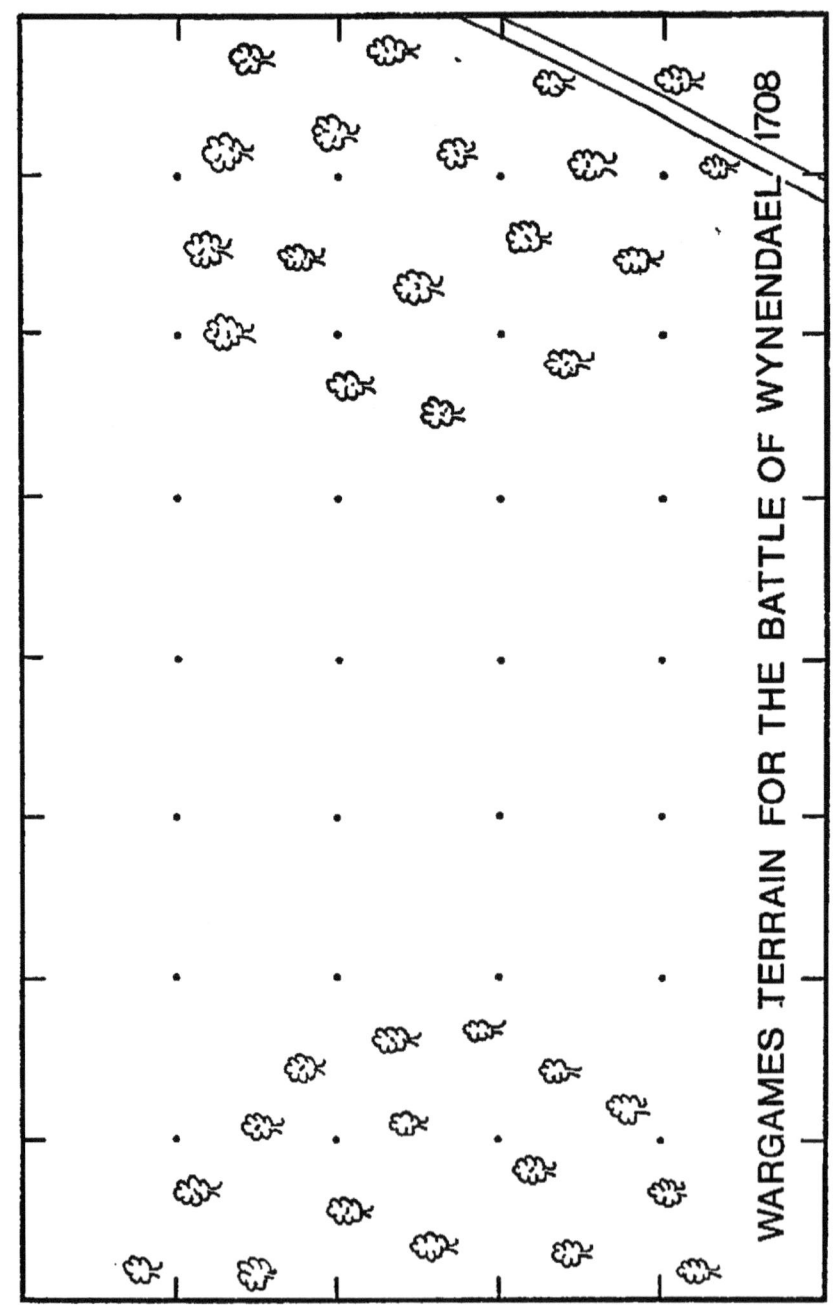

WARGAMES TERRAIN FOR THE BATTLE OF WYNENDAEL 1708

Construction of the terrain

The bulk of the battle took place in the defile between the woods, which sheltered Webb's flanking regiments. As a Military Possibility might cause the French to go in after them, the woods should be constructed to allow for this eventuality. They should be represented by large sheets of irregularly cut hard-board, painted dark green, their edges irregularly lined with trees. On the bottom right-hand corner of the terrain you could mark in the road over which Webb reroutes his convoy. This road can be shown and possible French attempts to intercept the convoy can be made on the map.

Stop! Read no further until you have deployed the forces and issued your detailed written orders.

The course of the actual historical battle.

Lottum's cavalry concluded their skirmishing and retired through their own infantry. Now a battery of 19 French guns opened a cannonade upon the closely formed Allied ranks that lasted for nearly two hours, but it had surprisingly little effect, for Webb had ordered his men to lie down. Then four lines of French infantry, supported by cavalry and dragoons, came forward and entered the defile between the woods, their flanks brushing the shrubbery. Suddenly, at a few yards' range, volleys of musketry poured out from both sides of the defile, causing the French flanks to recoil and reel back on their centre. Dragoons came forward in support and the infantry rallied, pressing forward so vigorously that they broke through two battalions of the first line. The gap was quickly filled from the second rank, however, and the French infantry were forced back. Eight Units of French foot then marched up and clouds of smoke filled the air as repeated musketry volleys assailed them from front, flank and rear until, in spite of the entreaties and blows of their officers, they broke and fled. The Allied infantry, advancing by platoons 'as if they were on exercise', fired volley after volley into them as they retired. Cadogan hastened up with a few squadrons of cavalry and considered charging the retreating enemy, but, realising that he was not strong enough to do so with any certain chance of success, stood off.

In a complete state of confusion the retreating French left more than 3,000 casualties on the ground and all their guns, which were recovered on the following day. Webb lost about 920 officers and men.

While the action was taking place, the convoy of wagons had been rerouted along a road to the rear of the wood, eventually arriving without loss two days later at Marlborough's camp.

The effects of this remarkable little action greatly relieved Marlborough, who only had sufficient ammunition at Lille to last four more days. 'If our convoy had been lost', he told Godolphin, 'the consequence must have been the raising of the siege.' Sir John Fortescue wrote: 'The signal incapacity displayed by the French Commander did not lessen the credit of Webb, and Wynendael was reckoned one of the most brilliant little affairs of the whole war'.

The Allied force, without artillery and with only a single squadron of cavalry, inflicted a resounding defeat upon a vastly superior French force because of its great superiority in discipline and tactics. The Allied fire was incomparably more deadly than that of the French, partly because the Allies had a better musket, but more because they fired by platoons whereas the French fired by ranks. With a maximum range of about 300 yards, the flintlock musket was so inaccurate that eighteenth-century European soldiers trained for volley-firing at 60-80 yards; in close formation they were able to hold off an attacking force by the sheer volume of their two aimed rounds per minute. The drilled and disciplined manner in which the Allies' superior musket was handled was superbly manifested in this overwhelming victory at Wynendael.

The Allied victory at Oudenarde, just over two months earlier, had given an enormous boost to Allied morale, and the French were discomfited by the aura that surrounded Marlborough's name. To both sides he was indisputably the greatest commander of his day.

Outline of the enemy's orders.

A die roll of 1, 2, 3 or 4 indicates the French commence the battle with a sustained artillery bombardment. After this, the cavalry will advance on a roll of 1, 2, 3 or 4; the infantry on 5 or 6. Each line will not assault until the previous line has been successful or has withdrawn. The French forces should ignore any infantry in the flanking woods until the concealed infantry have opened fired. After such infantry have revealed themselves, a roll of 1 in any turn means the French commit several units of infantry into the woods to protect the flanks of their main attack between the woods.

Ratings of the Commanders and Military Possibilities

Of the commanders in the field at Wynendael, Generals Cadogan, Webb and Lottum are 'above average', while de la Mothe should be rated 'below average'.

The events leading up to the battle can be marked on a scale-map covering an area of about twelve miles from north to south, with Roulers in the south, Ichtegem and Wynendael in the north and Thourout in the middle. The normal marching speed of infantry of this period was about ten miles per day (cavalry about double that), although Webb's infantry could march to the battle area at 'forced' march rate of fifteen miles per day, penalised by an agreed percentage (perhaps 10 per cent or less) dropping out en route.

The Wynendael position bore a strong resemblance to Agincourt, where in 1415 Henry V, with a force the same size as Webb's, overwhelmingly defeated a French army about as strong as de la Mothe's. Webb improved upon Henry V's dispositions by placing concealed troops so as to take the on-coming French in flank. The Allies were in an unflankable position possessing all the cohesive merits of the defensive square, plus the ability to bring maximum firepower to bear. The French cavalry charge at Wynendael was as unsuccessful as the charge of the French knights at Agincourt.

The cannonade lasts for a period in the wargamers' time-scale equivalent to two hours, and allowances must be made for Webb's tactic of ordering his troops to lie down when assessing casualties. The first line of the French infantry attack might have been composed of 1 regiment, other regiments subsequently following in line, or the 34 French infantry battalions may have attacked in battalion or even regimental columns—important factors from a wargaming point of view. On receiving fire, the French will check their state of morale, and then continue to advance or retreat, perhaps in disorder. If the entire front line is formed of 1 battalion and its morale is bad, that complete line will retire, with detrimental effects upon the lines behind it. However, if the attack is made in column, 1 battalion-column may be forced to withdraw but there will be others whose state of morale will be good enough to permit them to advance.

As at Agincourt, the restricted terrain prevents the French commander from bringing all his forces into action simultaneously; his formations are compressed and crowded upon each other in any case as they funnel into the wooded defile. They also then come within range of the troops posted in the woods on either flank. There is nothing harder to portray on the table-top than concealment, and the French 'commander' is well aware that there are troops concealed on his flanks; but, for an accurate simulation of the Wynendael skirmish, he must advance as though he were unaware of that fact. Such a course, however, will almost certainly lead to defeat; so a compromise is required.

A rudimentary simulation of an ambush on the wargames table is to allot one plastic counter of the same basic colour as the uniform of the man concerned for each figure involved in the ambush. Webb conceals say a dozen red-coated British infantrymen in the woods on his right flank, represented by that number of red counters similarly concealed in the table-top forest. The French may, when within 6 inches of a visible counter, deviate or take some form of offensive action, and it has to be decided whether the ambusher or the attacker fires first. In their excitement the ambushers may fire too soon, or they may be steady enough to hold their fire until the oncoming French are at point-blank range. When the ambushers fire into them, the packed French ranks recoil towards the centre, so that all units affected by this flank fire must test their morale.

The French Dragoons rallying and supporting the infantry will raise their morale, and they may join in a mêlée with the Allied infantry formations. In the table-top reconstruction the result of this mêlée may turn in favour of the French, so that they force back the entire British line rather than breaking through the first line of 2 battalions but being forced back as the gap is filled from the second line, as occurred in 1708. The French were, in fact, thrown back in some confusion, and de la Mothe sent forward 8 more lines of infantry, who, in a wargame, would need to test their morale—undoubtedly they would have been shaken by the repulse of their comrades. When Webb's Allied infantry drove them back in panic, the French infantry's morale had reached its lowest ebb.

When the French are fleeing in disorder, Webb orders his infantry to advance, and they move forward by platoons, each firing in support of the other. A Military Possibility might disagree here. Did the Allied infantry have sufficient ammunition left to continue firing or had they expended it all? Infantry had 23-30 ready-prepared cartridges, and in a lengthy action commanders had to make sure that their troops did not fire off their ammunition too quickly. This factor can be simulated in a wargame by allocating, say, 8 rounds of ammunition per man at the start of the battle and then noting the number of volleys, so that, as in real-life, the careful commander must exercise fire control.

The last phase of the battle brings Cadogan with what Fortescue calls 'a few squadrons of cavalry' but, probably because of the uncommitted French squadrons hovering around at the rear of the battlefield, no pursuit is pressed home. This presupposes that our table-top simulation has followed the same course as the original battle—but what if the boot is on the other foot and the Allies are in dire straits? Now Cadogan's cavalry might be needed to aid a sorely pressed Webb, and it would be necessary to define exactly how many were Cadogan's 'few' squadrons. They could move on the map, and arrive on the wargames table at the right moment; Chance Cards could be used to determine if any of them fall by the wayside.

Other variations are open to the French 'commander' who, with hindsight, will not wish to follow the losing tactics of Count de la Mothe. For example, French cavalry could move on the map to intercept the convoy on its circuitous route away from the scene of action; or Webb could weaken his force at Wynendael by detaching infantry to guard the convoy—there is little information as to the escort but obviously the convoy was not unguarded. Both these Military Possibilities, however, would turn the battle into just another wargame.

Notes

These notes – and those to the other chapters – are not exhaustive lists of all the suitable figures, rules and books that are available, and only figures manufactured and/or sold in the United Kingdom are listed. Website, rather than postal, addresses have been given wherever possible.

Wargame Figures suitable for Wynendael

2mm

Irregular Miniatures have suitable models in their Horse and Musket range and also offer ready-made Marlburian armies.

6mm or 1/300 scale

Baccus has War of Spanish Succession troops in its Early 18th century range.

Heroics and Ros have a Marlborough period range.

Irregular Miniatures Restoration/League of Augsberg and 18th century ranges have suitable figures.

10/12mm

Irregular Miniatures has suitable 18th century figures.

Old Glory UK Grand Scale has a Marlburian range.

Pendraken has a Marlburian range.

15mm

Essex Miniatures European Armies 1660-1745 has suitable figures.

Irregular Miniatures League of Augsberg and Marlburian ranges have many suitable figures.

Miniature Figurines has suitable figures in their Marlburian and Great Northern War range.

20mm

Plastic figures suitable for the War of Spanish Succession are listed on the website www.plasticsoldierreview.com/Index.aspx; other figures from the Great Northern War and Seven Years' War lists might also prove useful to recreate Wynendael.

Irregular Miniatures Restoration/League of Augsberg and Marlburian ranges have many suitable figures.

25/28mm

Foundry Miniatures have a Marlburian range.

Irregular Miniatures have a Marlburian range.

Miniature Figurines has a Marlburian range.

Old Glory Age of Reason ranges contain troops for the Wars of Marlborough.

Wargame Rules suitable for Wynendael

Black Powder: Battles with model soldiers in the age of the musket, Rick Priestley and Jervis Johnson, Warlord Games
The freewargamerules website has several sets of rules for Marlburian warfare.
Horse, Foot and Guns, Phil Barker, Wargames Research Group,
Donald Featherstone's Lost Tales, History of Wargaming Project, contains rules for the Ancient period.
The Junior General website has simple rules in scenarios for Blenheim and Ramillies that could be used to fight Wynendael.

Marlborough s'en va-t-en guerre : a full set of campaign & battlefield rules for the War of the Spanish Succession, Realistic Modelling Services
Polemos War of the Spanish Succession, Baccus6mm

Further Reading

The British Army 1660-1704, John Tincey, Osprey Men At Arms 267
Louis XIV's Army, Rene Chartrand, Osprey Men At Arms 203
Marlborough's Army 1702-1711, Michael Barthorp, Osprey Men At Arms 97
The French Wars 1667-1714: The Sun King at War, John A. Lynn, Osprey Essential History 34

The historical battlefield map

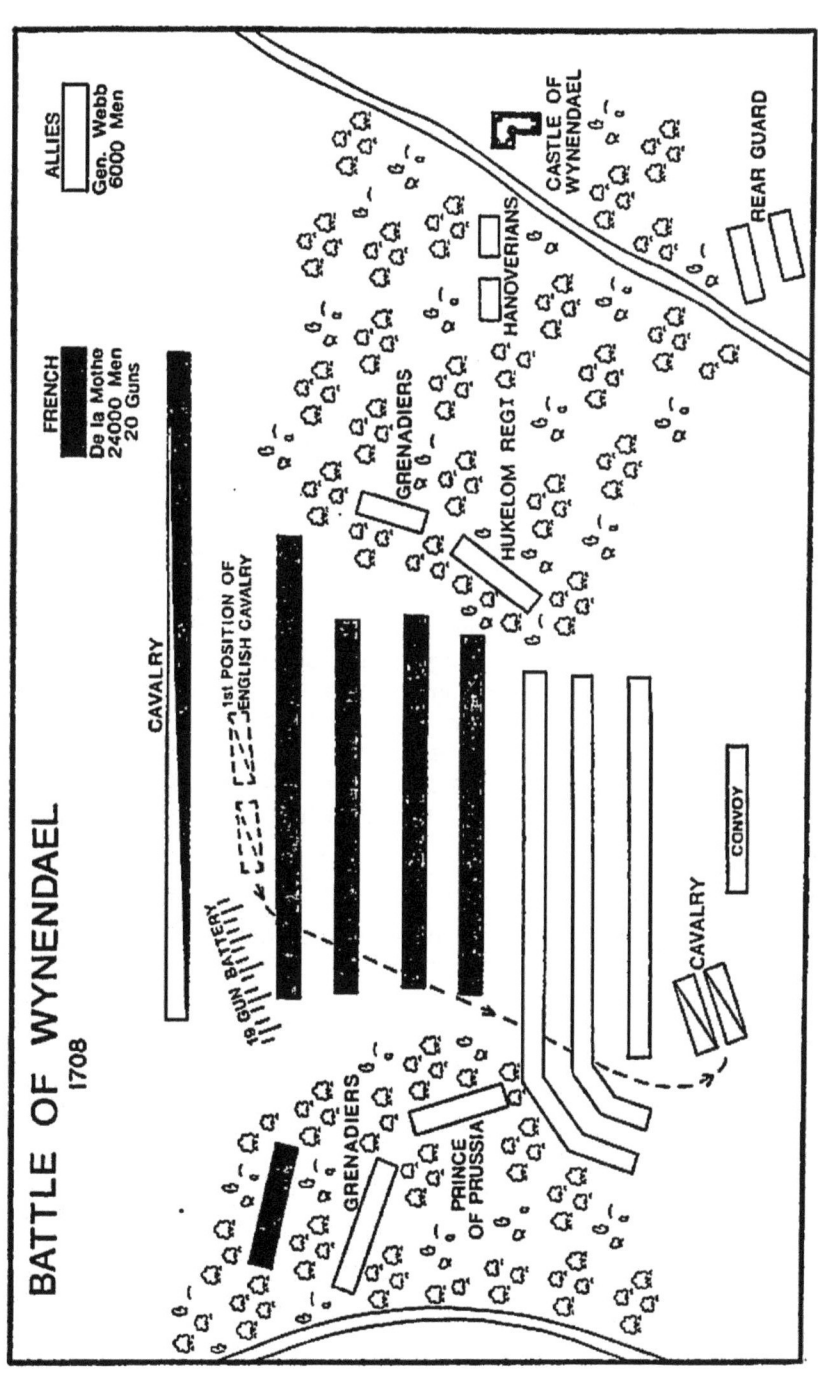

6. The Battle of Prestonpans

21 September 1745

You are Sir John Cope[18], commanding an ill-trained army waiting for the Jacobites.

Historical Background

THIS ENGAGEMENT was fought during the Jacobite rebellion between the Highland army of Charles Stuart, the Young Pretender, and an English force commanded by Sir John Cope who, following the fall of Edinburgh, marched hurriedly from Dunbar to bring the Jacobite army to action. On 20 September 1745 the two armies found themselves about ¾ mile apart and, aware of the Highlanders' headlong methods of attack, Cope took up a defensive position at the eastern end of a flat and featureless tract of land lying to the north of the higher ground around Tranent.

Friendly Forces Cope had about 3,000 ill trained and ill-disciplined troops, including 6 squadrons of dragoons, whose horses were unsuitable for their role, being unaccustomed to firearms and frequently taking fright and bolting. His lack of Regular artillerymen greatly handicapped Cope; although the Highlanders had become accustomed to artillery, its value was more than demonstrated by Cumberland at Culloden, and its effective use would have heightened morale at Prestonpans, where the English had six 1½ pounder guns and 6 mortars.

Enemy Forces Prince Charles' force numbered about 2,550 infantry and 40 mounted men, but lacked artillery. The Highlanders were armed with a broadsword, a dirk and a target (a small circular shield); some had pistols and a few had muskets. Their strength lay in their frightening headlong charge.

---

[18] Sir John Cope (born 1690), British general and MP, had served in the War of the Spanish Succession and the War of Austrian Succession. Cope was appointed Knight of the Bath (KB) for his performance in battle in Germany during the latter.

As Commander-in-Chief, Scotland, he was in command of the Government forces at the Battle of Prestonpans

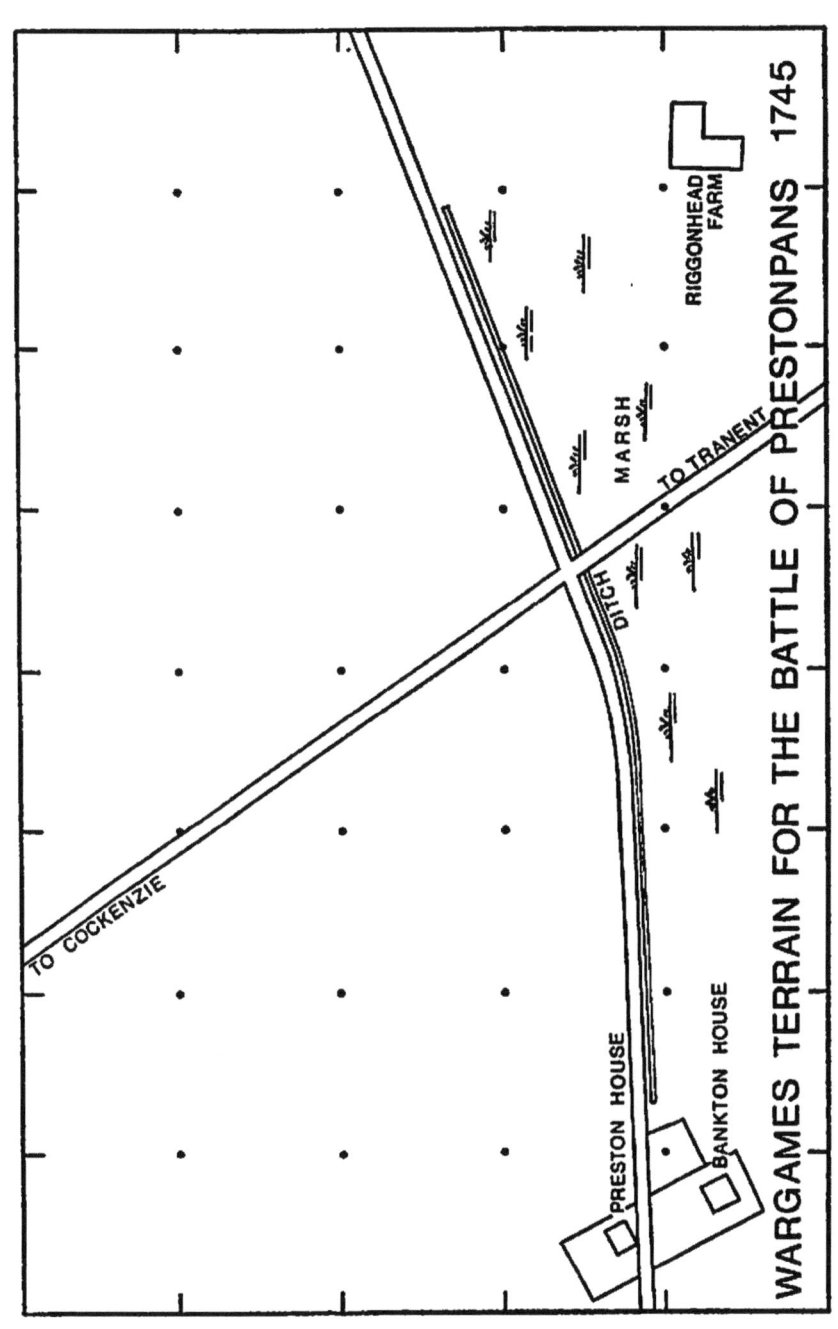

Construction of the terrain

This terrain must allow for Cope to take up his original position along the road running from Preston House to the crossroads, for the Highlanders to come on to the table in the later stages of their outflanking march, and for Cope to take up a new position facing his flank. There must be sufficient room for the action that follows to take place in the top right-hand third of the terrain, in an area bordered by the roads to Cockenzie and the ditch. It is not essential to have the buildings on the table, but they provide areas which might be affected by Military Possibilities, besides giving interest to the appearance of the terrain. The ditch and marsh, while not playing a vital part in the historical conflict, could, with some Military Possibilities, take on some importance. This is not a difficult terrain to make, as it is completely flat.

Stop! Read no further until you have deployed the forces and issued your detailed written orders.

The course of the actual historical battle

The redcoats had muskets with bayonets, but their slowness in reloading brought disaster at Prestonpans, though the lesson was learnt in time for Culloden, where the English infantrymen, formed in three ranks and firing one rank at a time, effectively thrust their bayonets in the unguarded sides of the Highlanders.

Anticipating an attack from the south, Cope positioned his men with his right flank towards the walls of Preston House. His artillery was posted all together on the left wing instead of being distributed along his line, since he only had some seamen-gunners from warships, who were frequently drunk, to man the guns, and they ran away at the start of the action.

The Highland army prepared for a fierce charge, but close examination of the ground revealed that any such attack was quite impracticable. Even at this stage there was disagreement between the army commanders, Lord George Murray and John O'Sullivan; there was mutual distrust, and much doubt from O'Sullivan when Lord George outlined a bold but simple plan for a night march round the east end of the morass to fall upon the enemy's open flank, after a local man had described a track that would bring them to the area.

In his initial position Cope attempted to shake the Highlanders with artillery fire, running two of his 1½ pounders forward to be loaded and fired by the seamen-gunners, but at a range of 800 yards they were ineffective. Similarly, during the night, Cope attempted to annoy the Highlanders by shelling their position, but abandoned the idea after a single mortar round revealed the inadequacies of the fuses.

Commanding a numerically superior force of Regular soldiers, Cope might be criticised for not attacking the Highlanders, though this would have exposed his army to the same disadvantages as would have accompanied an attack by the Highlanders in the opposite direction. None of Cope's troops had seen previous action, and they could only be kept in hand in a defensive position; the ground was suited for cavalry and the Highlanders had none.

Shortly before 4 am, led by the local guide, the Highland army began to move slowly north-eastwards down the ridge; the column passed safely through the narrow defile close to the farm of Riggonhead, where it could have been intercepted by Cope's cavalry scouts. Dawn came as it traversed the morass, and despite the low morning mist it was discovered by patrolling Dragoons, who galloped back to raise the alarm. Passing over the narrow plank bridge that crossed the 4 foott ditch bounding the morass on the north, the Highland vanguard debouched on to the plain about 1,000 yards to the east of Cope's left flank. The head of the column marched on towards Cockenzie until it was estimated that the rear of the front line troops were clear of the marsh but, when the van turned left to form line it was separated from the rear by a gap that was not closed until just before the attack began.

Receiving the dragoons' report of the Highlanders' movement, Cope had an alarm gun fired to recall his patrols, and then manoeuvred his army to face the enemy, with the infantry wheeling left by platoons and marching off northwards, roughly parallel to the line of march of the Highlanders. Halting, the infantry turned right into lines three deep and faced east, with their left towards Cockenzie and their right protected by the large ditch. Drawn up from left to right were 9 companies of Murray's, 8 of Lascelles', 2 of Guise's and 5 of Lee's; they were separated from the artillery on their right by a space sufficient for 2 squadrons of cavalry. With mortars on their right, the guns, 6 feet apart, were in line with the infantry, and were guarded by 100 men of Murray's Regiment on the right of the line. Two deep, a squadron each of Gardiner's and Hamilton's Dragoons, with one of each in reserve, moved up to take position in the line; Hamilton's formed up as ordered but Gardiner's formed up in rear of the artillery, where there was little room, for this space had been taken up by the infantry out-guards, who had returned but did not have time to rejoin their regiments.

The Highlanders' front line began to advance and Cope, seeing that his left wing was outflanked, ordered two guns to be sent over from the right, but the frightened civilian drivers rode off with the limber horses, closely followed by the seamen-gunners who were supposed to work the guns.

As the sun rose, Lord George Murray ordered the Highlanders of the left wing to advance; they moved forward unevenly, their left well in advance of their right wing. Discarding their plaids, and with bonnets pulled low over their brows, they rushed forward screaming, terrifying the makeshift artillerymen, who fled. The two officers left to handle the guns managed to fire 5 of the 1½ -pounders and all 6 of the mortars, although many of the defective shells burst ineffectively. Had the guns been manned by Regular artillerymen their effect might have been decisive, because even this spasmodic fire caused a momentary tremor in the Highland ranks.

The Highlanders broke into separate bodies, the largest group making straight for the artillery. Hamilton's Dragoons were ordered to charge them in the flank and their commander, Colonel Whitney, led them out to within pistol shot of the Highlanders, but suddenly all the horsemen turned and ran, leaving Whitney alone. The artillery guard left their ground and crowded in a confused mass behind the guns they were supposed to be guarding and, when instructed to support the Dragoons, refused to go forward. Quickly their officers reorganised them into a regular front rank but, after delivering an ineffectual volley, they gave way as both they and the artillery were overrun. Gardiner was ordered to charge but, alarmed by the artillery guards falling back, his entire squadron turned and fled.

On the extreme right the advancing Highlanders maintained their line in very orderly fashion and, outflanking Cope's left, swung obliquely inwards, and with their musket fire caused casualties in Hamilton's other squadron, which galloped off in a panic-stricken body.

Deserted by the cavalry and exposed to the full fury of the Highlanders' attack, the unfortunate infantry wavered, in spite of the efforts of Cope and other officers to steady it. The foot soldiers were broken into from right to left by successive waves , hacking and stabbing their way forward, and became a flying rabble. Cope and the Lords Loudon and Home tried to round up the dragoons, who were now crowded into the narrow defiles south of Preston House, and succeeded in turning about 450 of them into a field and reforming them. But then a body of Highlanders appeared and the cavalrymen refused to attack; so, realising that nothing could be expected of their men, Cope and the rest of his officers rode off at their head, this being the only way of keeping them together.

Scarcely more than five minutes had elapsed from the first onslaught on Cope's army to its rout. Cope's infantrymen, in their tight clothing and heavy equipment, had little chance of escape, and all but 170 of them were killed or captured. In all, Cope lost 200 killed and about 500 wounded, and 1,500 of his men were taken prisoner. Highland casualties were 30 killed and 75 wounded.

Although Prestonpans was a decisive Jacobite victory, it played a vital part in their defeat and destruction at Culloden by persuading Charles Stuart that his Highlanders were invincible.

Outline of the enemy's orders.

The Jacobite's army sets off on its outflanking manoeuvre, however the timing is crucial. Therefore roll a die; 1 or 2, Cope can start to move his army after 1 move, 3 or 4 after 2 moves, 5 or 6 after 3 moves.

The Jacobite Army may not have launched a coordinated attack. Therefore roll a die for each clan when the 'Highland' charge is made; 1, 2, 3 or 4 then the clan advances that turn, 5 or 6 re-roll the following turn.

Ratings of the Commanders and Military Possibilities

Cope was 'below average', O'Sullivan 'average' and Lord George Murray 'above average'. The British unit commanders (Murray, Lascelles, Guise, Lee, Gardiner and Hamilton) were all 'below average'.

Making Lord George Murray an 'above average' commander balances the numerical deficiency of the Highlanders, besides ensuring that their morale is sufficiently high to undertake the vital outflanking movement. A Military Possibility can represent the known discord between Lord George Murray and John O'Sullivan by the occasional drawing of Chance Cards to control the cohesiveness of the Highland army.

The key to the battle is the race between the Highlanders to deploy and charge while Cope, perhaps after a momentary check through surprise, turns his army left and marches it to face its new position. This march must be done in a reasonably formal fashion, as these were the days of unthinking soldiers moving *en masse* in response to rigid orders. In a sense the situation is akin to a Colonial battle in which fleet-footed natives outmanoeuvre their slower opponents and then, backed by the superior morale given them by their frightening weapons and courage, charge overwhelmingly upon their more civilised enemy.

If Cope's cavalry scouts had discovered the advancing Highlanders in the Riggonhead defile and fought a minor delaying action, the English commander could have had more time to reposition his army. This is a Military Possibility that could make a difference to the battle with only small amendment to reality. A delay advantageous to Cope could be caused by the Highland army funnelling in to cross the plank bridge over the 4 foot ditch.

The inadequacies of Cope's artillery, both in gunners and defective fuses, should be reflected by local rules giving a low standard of morale to the gunners and little effectiveness to the missiles. Cope's artillerymen fled at the sight of the enemy—a Military Possibility could give them a slight chance of staying and firing their guns. Assuming that they follow historical precedence and run, it must be decided how effective was the fire of the two officers who remained. It has been noted that even these despairing efforts caused a momentary tremor in the Highlanders' ranks so that sustained artillery fire might well have reduced their morale and checked their charge.

Cope's infantry out-guards, 300 strong, were made up of detachments from each regiment and, as we have said, did not have time to rejoin their own units, crowding out Gardiner's Dragoons instead. It is feasible to assume that, lacking the esprit-de-corps of being with their own units, this force had a low standard of morale.

As in real life, attacks on the wargames table may be held off by weight of firepower. The morale of the firers affects their aim and their ability to remain steady and hold their fire until the enemy are close upon them. Shaky, ill disciplined and badly trained troops will fire off a volley at long range, and then reload their muskets so as to give the onrushing enemy another volley before they make contact. Vital aspects of this battle could be the inability of Cope's infantry to hold its fire, or the possibility of its reloading to get in two volleys. There are a number of Military Possibilities here worthy of exploration.

Well handled cavalry could be extremely effective against the Highlanders, who did not possess any horsemen, but Cope's cavalrymen, with their low morale, refused to attack. A Military Possibility could give them a higher rating, so that some of them will charge, which could affect the outcome of the battle. Cope's inability to rally his infantry could be changed by a Military Possibility that gave him a slight chance of doing so; or he might induce his reformed cavalry to charge from the area of the Preston House—a determined cavalry charge on the disordered and uncohesive Highlanders from there could have swung the battle in his favour.

This action was largely decided by morale—low among the English soldiers and high among the Highlanders. The former were afraid of the Highlanders and their fearsome onslaughts with the claymore. These charges can only be turned back on the wargames table by firepower *before* they make contact; once they force a mêlée their impetus (which can be represented by assuming that two Highlanders are the equal of three British infantrymen) will ensure success.

Notes

These notes – and those to the other chapters – are not exhaustive lists of all the suitable figures, rules and books that are available, and only figures manufactured and/or sold in the United Kingdom are listed. Website, rather than postal, addresses have been given wherever possible.

Wargame Figures for Prestonpans
2mm

Irregular Miniatures have regulars in their Horse and Musket range, but no models suitable for Jacobite clansmen – how would one paint tartan in this scale, anyway!

6mm or 1/300 scale

Adler Miniatures has Seven Years' War Austrians and Prussians, some of which could be painted as British troops.

Baccus has Seven Years War British troops, but no Jacobites; perhaps one could use Highlanders from the English Civil War range.

Heroics and Ros have only Prussian and Austrian Seven Years' War troops, but perhaps their Marlburian British and English Civil War Highlanders could be used.

Irregular Miniatures have British regulars and Highlanders in their 18th century range.

10/12mm

Irregular Miniatures have suitable British troops and Jacobite clansmen in their 18th century range.

Miniature Figurines now owned by Caliver Books of Nottingham has

Pendraken has Seven Years' War British and Jacobite ranges.

15mm

Essex Miniatures European Armies 1660-1745 has suitable figures for British troops and Highlanders.

FreiKorp 15 has a Charles Stuart figure and Jacobites in its Seven Years' War (!) ranges, together with a Duke of Cumberland, staff officers and British troops that could portray the forces at Prestonpans.

Irregular Miniatures have British regulars in their French and Indian Wars range, but no Jacobites.

Magister Militum War of the League of Augsburg range has Highlanders that would be suitable for Jacobites, but the regular infantry are not Seven Years' War period.

Miniature Figurines has Jacobites 1688-1746; Government forces may be found in the Seven Years' War range.

20mm

The website www.plasticsoldierreview.com/Index.aspx lists only three sets – all Scottish Highlanders – under Jacobite Rebellions. The Government forces must be recruited from the Seven Years' War lists.

Irregular Miniatures have Jacobites in their Marlburian range; British regulars may be found in the French and Indian War range.

25/28mm

Foundry Miniatures have Seven Years' War British troops; suitable figures for Jacobite Highlanders are in the English Civil War range.

Miniature Figurines has Seven Years' War British troops, but no Jacobites.

Old Glory has a Jacobite Rising range with troops for both sides.

Wargame Rules suitable for Prestonpans

Black Powder: Battles with model soldiers in the age of the musket, Rick Priestley and Jervis Johnson, Warlord Games
De Bellis Magistrorum Militum, Phil Barker, Wargames Research Group, 2010.
Donald Featherstone's Lost Tales, History of Wargaming Project, contains rules for the Ancient period.
The freewargamerules website has numerous sets of rules for the Seven years' War which could be adapted for Prestonpans.
The Junior General website has a Jacobite Uprising: Prestonpans 1745 scenario complete with simple rules.

Further Reading

Cassell's Battlefields of Britain & Ireland, Richard Brooks, Weidenfield & Nicolson (2005).
Culloden 1746: The Highland Clans' Last Charge, Peter Harrington, Osprey Campaign 12
Highland Clansman 1689-1746, Stuart Reid, Osprey Warrior 21
The Battle of Prestonpans 1745, Martin Margulies, NPI Media Group, 2007
The Jacobite Rebellions 1689-1745, Michael Barthorp, Osprey Men At Arms 118

The historical battlefield map

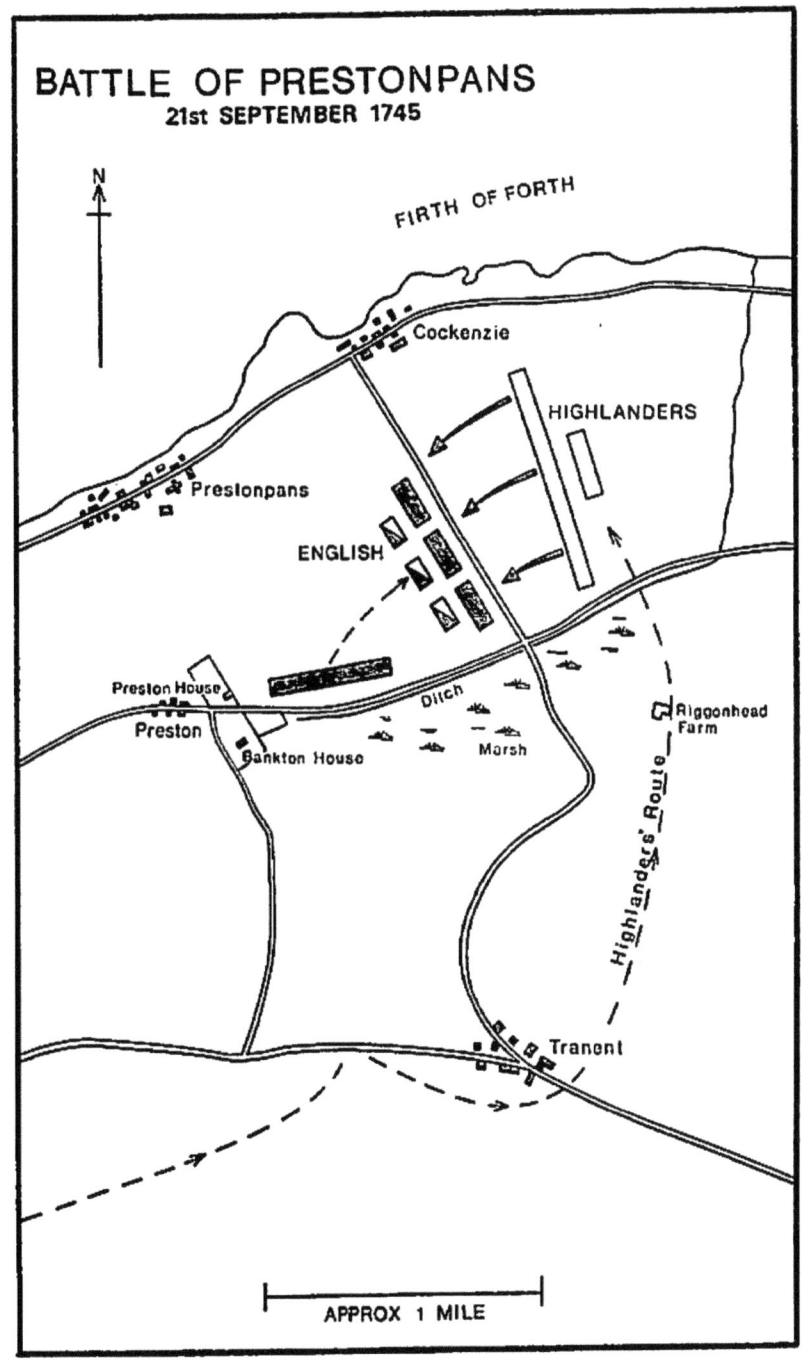

7. The Battle of Guilford Courthouse

15 March 1781

You are General Cornwallis[19], commanding the British forces.

Historical Background and forces deployed

THIS ENCOUNTER took place during the American Revolution (1775-83) between an American force under General Nathanael Greene and a British army under General Cornwallis. The contrast between the rigidity of the British Regular forces and the loose and unorthodox tactics of the American Militia makes for unusual but fascinating table-top battling.

British forces 1,900 men and 3 guns.

Cornwallis' army was much better organised, disciplined and trained than the American, and his men, perhaps the best British forces in

---

[19] Charles Cornwallis (born 31 December 1738), The Earl Cornwallis, was born into an aristocratic family and well-educated. He was commissioned Ensign in the 1st Foot Guards in 1757, and served in Germany in the Seven Years' War. Upon his father's death in 1762 he became Earl Cornwallis and entered the House of Lords. Promoted to Colonel of the 33rd Foot in 1766, he next saw military action in 1776 in the American War of Independence, participating in the first siege of Charleston, the battles of Long Island, the Brandywine, Germantown and Monmouth. He then returned to England to care for his wife Jemima, who died in 1779.

Cornwallis returned to America in July, 1779, to play a central role as the lead commander of the British 'Southern strategy'. Clinton and Cornwallis began a second siege of Charleston in spring 1780, which resulted in the surrender of Benjamin Lincoln's Continental forces. Clinton then returned to New York, leaving Cornwallis in command in the south. Cornwallis was tasked with seeking an outright victory over the rebels. His forces were limited by the need to keep large British force in New York to shadow Washington.

In August 1780 Cornwallis' forces met the larger but untried army of Horatio Gates at the Battle of Camden, where they inflicted heavy casualties and routed part of the force. This served to effectively clear South Carolina of Continental forces, and was a blow to rebel morale. This victory added to Cornwallis' reputation, though the rout of the American rebels had as much to do with the failings of Gates as it did to his skill. Cornwallis then began to advance north into North Carolina. Attempts by Cornwallis to rally Loyalist support were dealt significant blows when a Ferguson's Loyalists were defeated at King's Mountain, only a day's march from Cornwallis' army, and another large detachment of his army was decisively beaten at Cowpens.

America, were veterans commanded by able experienced officers. Their right wing under Major-General Leslie consisted of Bose's Hessian Regiment and Fraser's Highlanders in the first line, with the 1st Guards in support; the left wing was formed of the 23rd and 33rd Regiments under Colonel Webster in the first line, with the Grenadiers and the 2nd Guards in support. A small corps of German Jagers and the Light Infantry was stationed in the wood to the left of the road, while Tarleton with the cavalry remained in the rear on the road. Cornwallis posted his 3 guns on the road itself; they could not move anywhere else because the woods restricted their field of fire

The British are positioned at the bottom of the hill and have been unable to gain much information from prisoners or the local residents. The American position is over the stream along the line of the nearest fence. One six pounder cannon is either side of the road.

American forces

North Carolina Militia of 3,000 men, a Virginia State regiment, a corps of Virginian eighteen-month men and recruits for the Maryland Line, giving a total of 4000-5000 men.

Construction of the terrain

This battle, being fought in three separate stages, requires the extensive area allowed by laying the terrain lengthways, with the stream on the 'bottom' baseline. From there a ridge 18 inches wide on its top, stretches right across the table, with three rail-fenced fields, each about 18 inches square. Because fighting has to take place amid the trees, the comparatively spacious areas of woodland must be made 'symbolic', by representing them with hardboard bases bearing occasional trees around their edges, the whole being the wood itself. The extensive ridge and hill are easy to form by draping grass-coloured cloth over shapes below. Considerable lengths of rail fence are required; this can be made from basket-weaving cane.

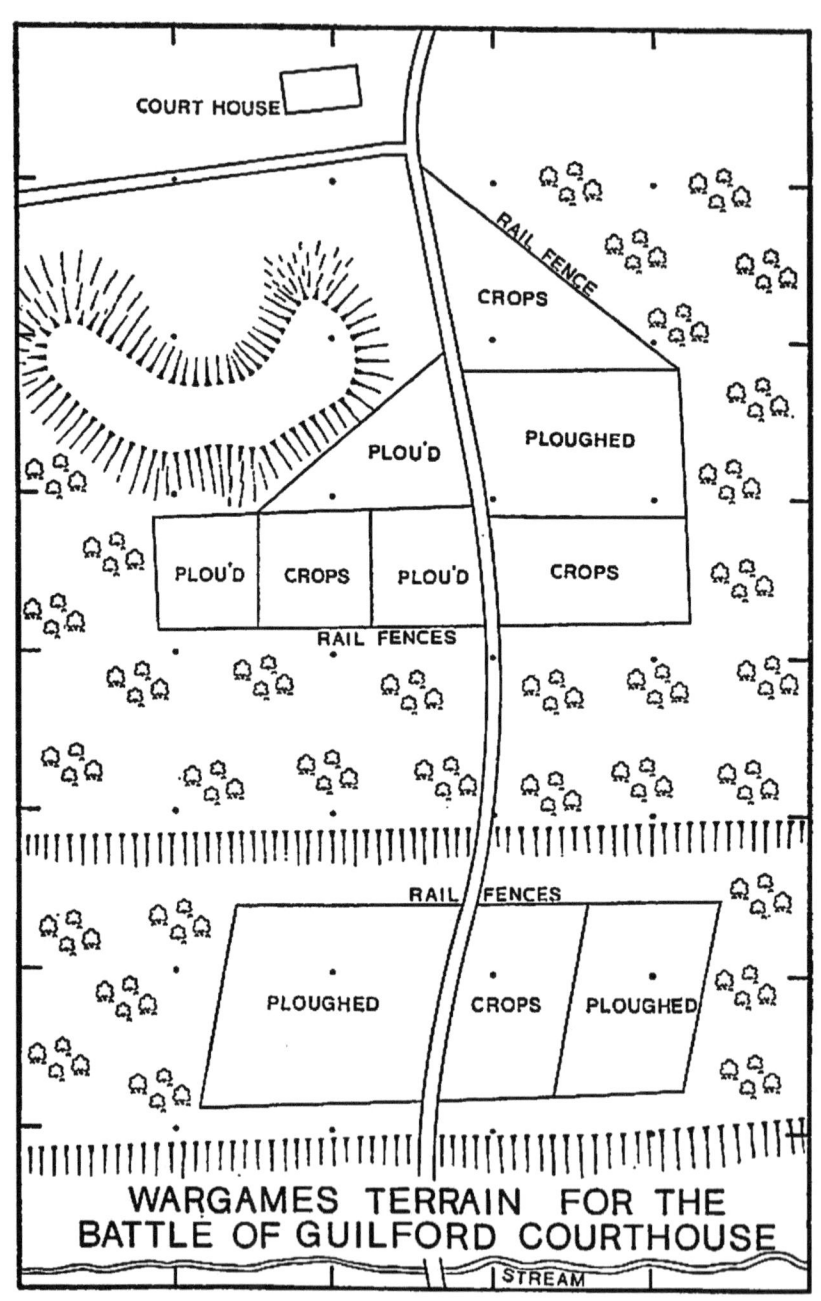

Stop! Read no further until you have deployed the forces and issued your detailed written orders.

The course of the actual historical battle.

This British victory marked the beginning of the end of the Revolution, because, by winning, Cornwallis so weakened his army that he lost the campaign in the southern colonies. Cornwallis had been pursuing Greene in the Carolinas in the hope of forcing an engagement, while Greene, wishing to avoid battle, was trying to draw the British as far as possible from their base. Early in March Greene collected reinforcements in Virginia that strengthened his force to about 5,500 men, moved westwards to Guilford Courthouse, within twelve miles of the British Army, and took up battle stations facing west in three lines 400 yards apart. At the head of a force of 1,900 men with 3 guns, Cornwallis marched at daybreak on 15 March. About four miles from Guilford Courthouse the advance cavalry of both armies met in a brief skirmish, and the Americans were driven back. Continuing the advance along the New Garden Road, the British crossed a small stream from which the ground rose gradually to an open space about 500 yards square, made up of three cultivated fields bordered by rail fences; the whole area forming a defile between thick copses of trees. Here, with an excellent field of fire and protected by the rail fences, Greene had drawn up his first line of 1,600 men. This line consisted of two brigades of North Carolina Militia, untrained soldiers without battle experience; two battle-experienced units — Lee's Legion (Regulars) and Campbell's Riflemen (frontiersmen from Virginia and the North Carolina mountains)—on their left; and Colonel William Washington's Regular Cavalry, some of the Delaware Regiment of Continentals and Lynch's Riflemen (veteran frontiersmen) on their right. Two 6-pdr guns in the centre on the road commanded the stream crossing.

About half a mile ahead of the clearing, in the woods that closed in on the road, Greene deployed his second line of about 1,000 Virginia Militia, untrained and inexperienced. Commanded by General Wilson on the right and General Stevens on the left, and officered by men who had served in the Continental army and had some battle experience, this second line was somewhat stronger than the first. All the troops of the second line were hidden in the woods on each side of the road, with picked marksmen behind them, ready to shoot any man who ran away.

Then came another open space of cultivated ground, made uneven by hollows, and 400 yards in rear of the second line, and rather to the west of the road, was a hill that formed the salient angle in the midst of the clearing around the Courthouse. Near the eastern edge of this clearing Greene drew up his third line of 1,450 Regular troops, the 2nd Virginia Brigade on the right and the 2nd Maryland Brigade on the left, with two 6-pounder guns between them. The right flank was unprotected, but the left flank, resting on the New Garden Road, was protected by artillery during the later stages of the battle. Both flanks of the first two lines were unprotected, but as the heavy woods forced the British to attack frontally, these exposed flanks were not a disadvantage.

The British force formed up under American artillery fire after crossing the stream at the foot of the hill, losing very few men, while the British artillery replied with an equally useless expenditure of ammunition. At about 1.30 pm the British troops advanced across the first clearing, amid a hail of fire from the invisible enemy in front and on the flanks, then charged with the bayonet. The North Carolina Militia melted away in panic, while Greene's two guns retired to take post near the road with the American third line. The British line halted and the flank battalions turned outwards to oppose the American riflemen, who were still pouring in a destructive fire from both sides. Bose's regiment wheeled off to the right flank, and the 1st Guards moved into the line to take their place next to the Highlanders; on the other wing the 33rd, with the Jagers and Light Infantry on their left, similarly wheeled off to the left flank and the Grenadiers and the 2nd Guards advanced to the left of the 23rd.

Slowly the redcoats pressed forward through the trees, driving the American riflemen back at the bayonet point; the cavalry of Lee and Washington fell back to conform. Bose's Regiment and the 1st Guards drove Lee and Campbell's left flank detachment backwards in a south-easterly direction in a struggle that completely detached them from the main course of the battle, their separate engagement only being broken off by the Americans at about the time the main conflict ended. The American right flank detachment briefly took position on the flank of the second line, and, when that retired, moved to the flank of the third line.

The attack proceeded east along the road and through the woods for about 400 yards until it struck the second line, where the rifle-armed Virginia Militia stubbornly held their ground, inflicting heavy losses on the advancing redcoats. Discipline and experience began to tell, and gradually Wilson's Brigade on the American right crumbled before the Light Infantry and Jagers, who were their equals at bush fighting. Stevens' Brigade, on Wilson's left, stood firm for a while, but finally the pressure told and both forces were pushed back until, reaching the road, they broke and retired in disorder through the wood to Greene's third line, protected from pursuit by Washington's cavalry retiring with them to the edge of the forest.

Entirely north of the road, Greene's last line was opposed by the British left wing, which was slowed up by heavy undergrowth and deep gullies. Led by Webster, the now considerably reduced 33rd, Light Infantry and Jagers, attacked the 1st Maryland Regiment, the finest battalion in the American Army, which steadily awaited the assault before pouring in a volley at close range and charging with the bayonet to drive the attackers back in disorder, with heavy loss. Although severely wounded, Webster drew his men off into the shelter of the woods and rallied them, supported by the three British 3-pounder guns, which advanced along the road and unlimbered on the rising ground at the edge of the forest, whence they kept up a steady and well directed fire.

While Webster's force was rallying, General O'Hara led the 2nd Guards and the Grenadiers, supported by the 23rd and the Highlanders, against the Maryland Brigade. Seemingly giving way before O'Hara's attack, the 2nd Maryland Regiment steadily withdrew as the Guards pressed them; suddenly Washington's cavalry galloped out of the woods to crash into the rear of the Guards, while the 1st Maryland Regiment flooded out of the undergrowth on to their left flank. Fighting fiercely, the Guards were utterly broken, and the danger of a wholesale retreat forced Cornwallis to order his artillery to fire grapeshot into the struggling mass, causing great losses to both Americans and British.

In the pause that followed Cornwallis reformed his line, rallying the 2nd Guards, who had been joined by the 1st Battalion ; Webster led up the 33rd, the Jagers and the Light Infantry on their left. Under the smoke of a volley Tarleton's Cavalry were sent in, to end the American resistance on the British right and then they moved across to join Bose's Regiment and press upon the Americans' left flank, while the remainder of the British line engaged their front.

Seeing that the day was lost, Greene ordered retreat, abandoning his guns; there was no pursuit by Cornwallis' exhausted troops. Casualties were 93 British killed and 439 wounded; 78 Americans killed and 183 wounded.

Outline of the enemy's orders.

The American defence is largely static and is described in some detail allowing the wargamer to position it on the table top in an historical manner. At the appropriate point the Maryland Regiment may advance on a roll of 1, 2, 3 or 4. The attack of Washington's cavalry is launched on a roll of 1, 2 or 3 at the same time. If it does not attack simultaneously, then roll again each subsequent until it does.

Ratings of the Commanders and Military Possibilities

Greene undoubtedly displayed strategical sense by fighting not to win but to cause Cornwallis such losses as to diminish his future prospects of victory. Greene is certainly an 'average' commander but could be classified as 'above average' here, though that rating would probably put victory completely beyond the reach of Cornwallis (himself an 'average' commander), with his considerably smaller army. Webster could be 'above average', as could Washington; and other commanders can be classified in relation to the performance of their units. It will be necessary to assess the varying states of morale and fighting ability of:

(a) the British Regulars,

(b) the Continental Regulars,
(c) the American Riflemen, and
(d) the American Militia.

This assessment could be handled after the manner of the Wargames Research Council's Ancient Rules, where Regulars, Barbarians and levies, etc, are given different values when building up an army. Otherwise, the British Regulars and the Continental Regulars could be considered as top-grade soldiers; the Riflemen classed as light infantry, but not given the high morale of the Regulars, because of lacking the Regulars' cohesion; and the militia given a low grading, both in morale and fighting ability, because of the likelihood of their fleeing the field without firing a shot.

With the numerically superior American army in positions of their own choosing and the British historically pledged to attack in rigid formations, the only manner in which this battle can be accurately simulated is to devise 'local' rules that balance these factors. The militia must check their morale state as soon as the British come within charge-move distance whenever they take fire and sustain casualties, or whenever they are brought in mêlée contact. The British Light Infantry and the Jagers be given the same powers of manoeuvrability as the American Riflemen.

The cohesion of the British units attacking in rigid formations should give them an increased morale bonus, or else it is doubtful whether they will ever get into mêlée contact, as they did in real life. In fact, the morale of the British should be capable of being raised to great heights; particularly in the case of the Guards who were driven off after being severely mauled by the high-rate Maryland Regulars, hit in the rear by cavalry and then flailed with grapeshot by their own artillery. They subsequently rallied and came forward again to the attack-a rare exploit, unlikely to occur under normal morale rules.

Military Possibilities can be devised to prevent the Militia from fleeing, to prevent the American second line from being pushed back to alter the withdrawal of Webster's men and even their subsequent rallying, and to allow the Guards to beat the Maryland Regiments and to turn and to fight off the cavalry rear attack, etc, etc. But the historical reality of Greene delaying action to maul his opponent, who consistently pushed forward indicates that the most realistic simulation will be achieved by judicious handling of the morale situation.

Notes
These notes – and those to the other chapters – are not exhaustive lists of all the suitable figures, rules and books that are available, and only figures manufactured and/or sold in the United Kingdom are listed. Website, rather than postal, addresses have been given wherever possible.

Figures suitable for Guilford Courthouse

2mm

Irregular Miniatures have 18th century regular troops in their Horse and Musket range.

6mm or 1/300 scale

Adler Miniatures has an American War of Independence range.

Baccus Seven Years' War troops could be painted for the American Revolution.

Irregular Miniatures 18th century range includes many suitable regular figures and also American Militia infantry.

10/12mm

Irregular Miniatures have regulars and American Militia in their 18th century range.

Old Glory UK Grand Scale has an American War of Independence range.

Pendraken has an extensive American War of Independence range.

15mm

Essex Miniatures has an American War of Independence range.

FreiKorp 15 has an American Revolution range.

Irregular Miniatures have a French and Indian/American Revolution range.

Miniature Figurines has an American Revolution range.

Peter Pig has a Washington's Army American Revolution range to accompany its rules for the period.

20mm

Airfix did produce two sets – Washington's Army and British Grenadiers – for the American Revolution.

Readers will find other suitable plastic figures for Guilford Courthouse at www.plasticsoldierreview.com/Index.aspx .

Irregular Miniatures have an American War of Independence range.

25/28mm

Foundry Miniatures have a large American War of Independence range.

Matchlock Miniatures, owned by Caliver Books of Nottingham has a small American War of Independence range.

Miniature Figurines has an American Revolution range.

Old Glory Age of Reason ranges have American War of Independence troops.

Perry Miniatures has an extensive American War of Independence range.

Wargame Rules suitable for Guilford Courthouse

Black Powder: Battles with model soldiers in the age of the musket, Rick Priestley and Jervis Johnson, Warlord Games
Washington's Army, Peter Pig Rules For the Common Man (RFCM)
Horse, Foot and Guns, Phil Barker, Wargames Research Group,
Donald Featherstone's Lost Tales, History of Wargaming Project, contains rules for the period.
The freewargamerules website has numerous sets of rules for battles of the American Revolution.
John Bull-Patriots, Company-level rules for the AWI and War of 1812, The Perfect Captain website
The Junior General website has an American Revolutionary War: Battle of Guilford Courthouse (1781) scenario, complete with *A Ruinous Victory* simple rules.
The World Turned Upside Down - Campaign & Battlefield Rules for the American War of Independence, Realistic Modelling Services
Warmaster

Further Reading

American Loyalist Troops 1775-1784, Rene Chartrand, Osprey Men At Arms 450
The American Provincial Corps 1775-84, Philip Katcher, Osprey Men At Arms 1
The American Revolution 1774-1783, Daniel Marston, Osprey Essential History 45
American War of Independence Commanders, Rene Chartrand, Osprey Elite 93
The British Army in North America 1775-1783, Robin May, Osprey Men At Arms 39
Continental Infantryman of the American Revolution, John Milsop, Warrior 68
The Cowpens-Guilford Courthouse Campaign, Burke Davis, University of Pennsylvania Press, 2002
General Washington's Army (2) 1779-83, Marko Zlatich, Osprey Men At Arms 290

Guilford Courthouse 1781: Lord Cornwallis's Ruinous Victory, Angus Konstam, Osprey Campaign 109
Long, Obstinate and Bloody; The Battle of Guilford Courthouse, Lawrence E. Babits and Joshua B. Howard, University of North Carolina Press, 2009
The Road to Guilford Courthouse: The American Revolution in the Carolinas, John Buchanan, John Wiley & Sons, 1999
With Zeal and Bayonets Only: The British Army on Campaign in North America, 1775-1783, Matthew H. Spring, University of Oklahoma Press, 2010

The historical battlefield map

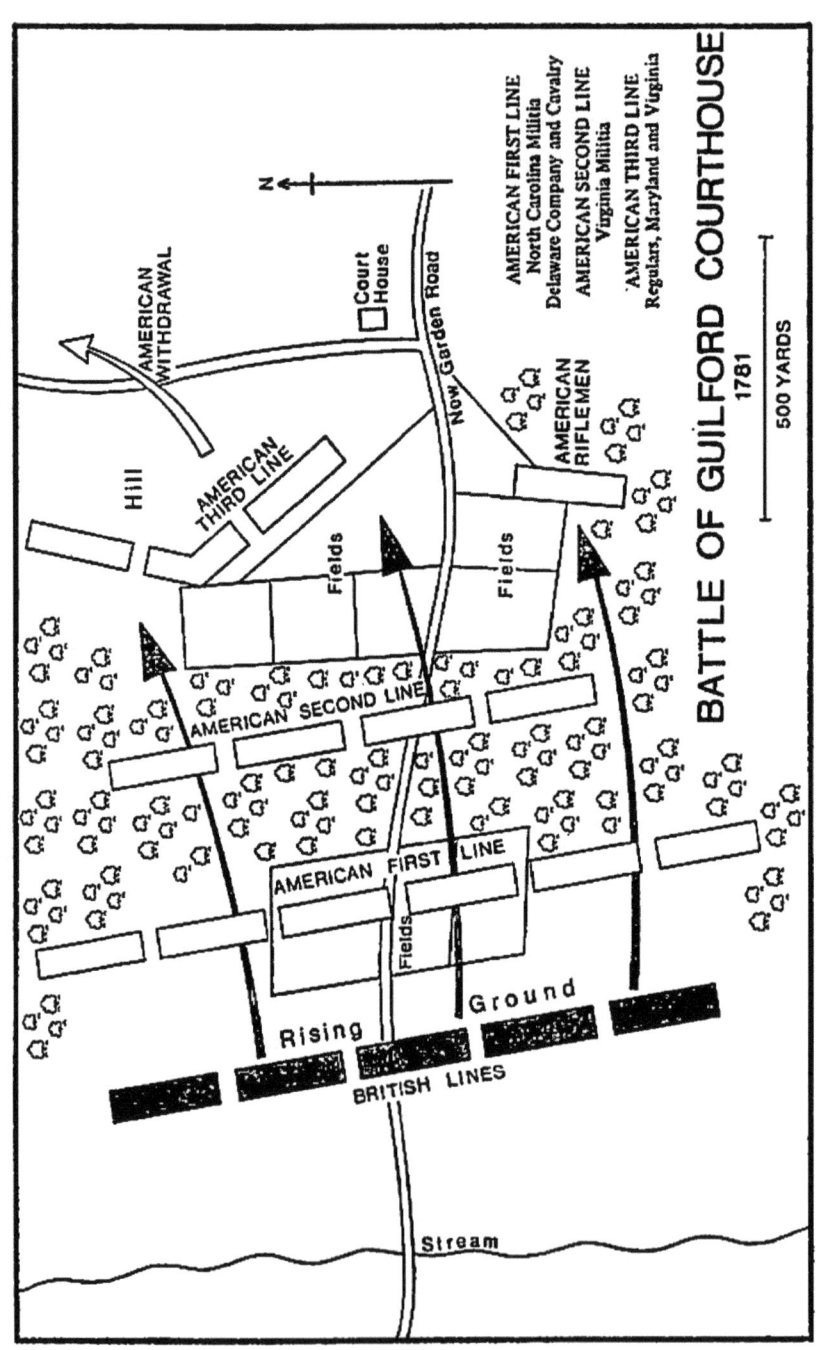

8. The Battle of Maida

4 July 1806

You are General Sir John Stuart[20], the British commander.

Historical Background and forces

THIS BATTLE was fought between a British force under General Sir John Stuart and a French army commanded by General Jean Reynier in Calabria during the Napoleonic Wars, undoubtedly the favourite period of wargamers, though most of the battles are too large for the wargames table. Maida, however, has all the typical features of the time.

On 1 July 1806 a British force under Sir John Stuart landed at the Bay of St Euphemia. It consisted of 7 battalions of infantry organised into an advance corps and 3 brigades; 2 of the battalions were composed of flank companies of various regiments and were experienced veterans, as were the 20th and 27th battalions, but the three remaining battalions comprised raw recruits. Totalling about 5,500 men, the force had eleven 4-pdr guns but no cavalry. The 20th battalion was detached to make a feint attack on Reggio.

Instead of gaining a tactical advantage by falling upon Reynier's troops while they were still dispersed, the British general remained stationary throughout 1, 2 and 3 July, because of the heavy surf, which made the landing of provisions difficult. Reynier gathered his force together during the three days, marching eighty miles from Reggio to

---

[20] Sir John Stuart (born 1759), son of a prominent Loyalist, educated at Westminster School, entered the 3rd Foot Guards in 1778, and almost immediately returned to America with his regiment. He was present at the siege of Charleston, the battles of Camden and Guilford Courthouse, and the surrender of Yorktown, returning a lieutenant.

Ten years later, as a captain, he was present with the Duke of York's army in the Netherlands and in northern France, taking part in the sieges and battles of the 1793 campaign. The following year, now commanding his battalion, he was present at Landrecies and at Tournay, and shared with his Guards in the discomforts of the retreat. As a brigadier-general he served in Portugal in 1796 and in Minorca in 1799. At Alexandria, in 1801, his handling of his brigade was commended in general orders, and a year later he became a major-general.

After two years in command of a brigade in Kent, Stuart went to the Mediterranean. The English and Russians were defending the Kingdom of Naples, but the Russians were withdrawn after Austerlitz and the British soon afterwards evacuated Italy. Naples fell to Massena, but Gaeta still held out for King Ferdinand, and was besieged by Masséna's main force. Stuart, who was in temporary command, realized the weakness of the French position in Calabria, and on the 1st of July 1806 swiftly disembarked all his available forces in the Gulf of Sant' Eufemia.

Maida, where he arrived on 3 July at the head of a force totalling 6,400, formed of 6 French infantry battalions (4,123), 1 Swiss infantry battalion (630), 2 Polish infantry battalions (937), 328 cavalrymen and a battery of horse artillery.

On the morning of 4 July the British force marched on to the plain of Maida in echelon of brigades with Kempt's Light Infantry leading the way, its right flank skirting the thicket that bordered the Lamato River; next came Acland's Brigade and then Cole's on the extreme left, while Oswald formed the reserve in rear of centre with 12 companies of infantry and 3 field guns. Manoeuvring in their front the French cavalry and horse artillery raised much dust, and the smoke of their guns and the British field pieces exchanging shots obscured the movements of the French infantry. When the dust subsided, Compere's Brigade of 2,800 veterans of the First Light Infantry and the 42nd of the Line advanced rapidly to the attack. On Compere's right was Peyri's Brigade of 1 Swiss and 2 Polish battalions (1,500) while on the right was Digonet's Brigade which included 1,250 infantrymen of the 23rd Light besides the cavalry and artillery.

Construction of the terrain

Maida has perhaps the simplest terrain of all the battles fought in this book, as it consists of a perfectly flat plain adorned by four areas of woodland. These are fairly extensive and, in at least one case, fighting or manoeuvring takes place within the confines of the trees. Thus, it is suggested that each area of woodland is 'symbolically' represented by an irregularly shaped piece of hardboard of the size indicated on the map, with a few trees dotted around its edges. The wood covers the entire area of the hardboard shape.

Reynier's losses were severe—more than 2,000 killed, wounded and prisoners compared with Stuart's 45 killed and 282 wounded.

Maida was a soldier's battle, won by the sheer merit and fortitude of individual units and their commanders, plus the superiority of British musketry training, and owing nothing to the skill of their commander, whom Fortescue described as 'cantering about all over the field . . . enjoying himself as a spectator but giving not a thought to the direction of the battle'. Fortescue also remarked that any one of the four British brigadiers —Cole, Kempt, Oswald and Ross—would have made a better commander than Stuart, and all made their mark later in the Peninsular War.

Outline of the enemy's orders.

The French will aim to overwhelm the numerically inferior British forces. Roll one die for each battalion: 1, 2 or 3 and it joins the initial advance. Roll for the horse artillery 1, 2 or 3 and it supports this advance. The Swiss unit may not be fired upon by the British on a roll of 4, 5 or 6 (do not roll until a British unit wishes to fire), until it fires or charges.

Ratings of the Commanders and Military Possibilities

Reynier, the French commander, does not show up at all well, and could be fairly given a 'below average' classification. His British opponent, Sir John Stuart, cannot be given better than 'average'—which makes it difficult for the numerically smaller, cavalry-less British force to achieve its historical success. It might be best to make both commanders 'average', and to give the British and French regiments morale and fighting classifications based on their performances in the battle.

British success was due to high morale coupled with the fact that the British musket threw a heavier bullet than the French, giving it a greater disabling power. The British fought in double and the French in triple ranks, so that every British musket was brought into action, thus presenting a greater front of fire—a 600-strong British battalion occupied a front of two hundred yards, whereas a battalion of 600 French soldiers covered only 135 yards, allowing the British to overlap the French by more than thirty yards each side and enabling them to fire on flanks as well as front. The British soldier had been carefully trained and strictly disciplined to obtain the maximum advantage from each shot. Both musket-balls and artillery fire could disable three French infantrymen, because of their formation, but the return fire could only disable two British.

All these factors must be reflected by suitably adapting rules and casualty-effect tables, together with the insistence that the British and French line formations are maintained throughout the battle. Tie British artillery would seem to have been better handled than the French, and a similar shading of the rules must reflect this.

Common to all horse-and-musket battles, the field soon became obscured by dust and smoke; at Maida the manoeuvring clouds to arise. This 'fog of war' is difficult to simulate, but there are helpful suggestions under 'Surprise' (at the start of this book).

One vital aspect of the battle was the conflict between the British and the French Light Infantry, which, if it is to be realistically simulated, must have the French charging precipitately (handled by an uncontrolled advance, as in Wargames Research Council Rules, or by an indifferent morale rating or by Chance Cards). As they go forward, the French are (1) fired on by the steady British Light Infantry, and (2) charged by them. Morale checks will be necessary to study the effects of these two actions, or their cumulative affects could be handled by a single morale check. A Military Possibility can be devised giving the French Light Infantry a chance of holding firm, but if history is repeated and they break, with the British Light Infantry in pursuit, then it has to be decided just how far and under how much control the pursuit is carried on. In the original battle the British Light Infantry were taken out of the action by their pursuit, which can be simulated, or else, by means of morale checks or Chance Cards, they can be rallied earlier and return to take part in the remainder of the battle.

The low morale of some units on the French side, such as Peyri's Polish Brigade, must be reflected in local rules to balance up the numerical inequality of the forces. Also, no self-respecting wargamer commander is going to allow the red-coated Swiss troops fighting for the French to approach and fire a volley upon a British unit that mistook them for comrades. While it may not have a vital affect upon the battle's result, the situation should be simulated, and could be resolved by Chance Cards. The British unit mastered their surprise to rally and drive the Swiss back, indicating high morale or a high rating for their commander.

Both Acland's and Cole's Brigades were, at various stages of the battle, held in check by French demonstrations with mounted chasseurs and horse artillery. Undoubtedly, in accordance with the practice of the times, they formed square under the threat of the cavalry, and were then assailed with

grapeshot by the artillery. Nevertheless, the British brigades were not broken nor did the French cavalry attack them—both features are not difficult to simulate on the wargames table.

A vital aspect of the battle was the arrival of the 20th Foot on Cole's left, after a march that can be carried out on the map, possibly affected by Chance Cards, so that they will arrive in time or too late. This battle is highly suitable for some interesting pre-conflict map-manoeuvring, although, if that is not carefully controlled, it may affect the accuracy of the reconstruction.

Notes
These notes – and those to the other chapters – are not exhaustive lists of all the suitable figures, rules and books that are available, and only figures manufactured and/or sold in the United Kingdom

are listed. Website, rather than postal, addresses have been given wherever possible.

Figures suitable for Maida

2mm

Irregular Miniatures have suitable models in their Horse and Musket range.

6mm or 1/300 scale

Adler Miniatures has suitable British and French figures.

Baccus has British and French troops.

Heroics and Ros has Napoleonic British and French.

Irregular Miniatures Napoleonics range has suitable figures for both sides.

10/12mm

Magister Militum has Napoleonic Wars British and French troops.

Miniature Figurines, now owned by Caliver Books of Nottingham has

Old Glory UK Grand Scale has British and French troops.

Pendraken have Peninsular British and French suitable for Maida.

15mm

Essex Miniatures has French 1806-12 and British 1800-13 figures suitable for Maida.

Irregular Miniatures have British and French troops.

Magister Militum has suitable British and French troops.

Matchlock Miniatures, owned by Caliver Books of Nottingham has a Peninsular War range with suitable British and French troops.

Miniature Figurines has suitable British and French figures in its Napoleonic range.

20mm

Airfix only made British, French and Prussian figures for the Battle of Waterloo. Today, HaT makes Peninsular War British Line and Light Infantry suitable for Maida. Readers will find these, and many plastic figures of French troops of the Napoleonic Wars listed and reviewed in depth on the website www.plasticsoldierreview.com/Index.aspx .

Irregular Miniatures have British and French troops, but mostly for the later Napoleonic campaigns.

25/28mm

Essex Miniatures has Peninsular War British and early Empire French.

Foundry Miniatures have extensive ranges of British and French troops.

Irregular Miniatures have British and French troops, but for the later campaigns.

Miniature Figurines has suitable British and French figures in its Napoleonic range.

Old Glory has suitable British and French figures in its Napoleonic ranges.

Perry Miniatures has a range of plastic and metal figures, but for Waterloo Campaign.

Wargame Rules suitable for Maida

Black Powder: Battles with model soldiers in the age of the musket, Rick Priestley and Jervis Johnson, Warlord Games
The freewargamerules website has numerous sets of rules for the Napoleonic Wars.
Horse, Foot and Guns, Phil Barker, Wargames Research Group,
Donald Featherstone's Lost Tales, History of Wargaming Project, contains rules for the Napoleonic period
The Junior General website has simple Napoleonic rules in a Salamanca 1812 scenario that could be used to fight Maida.
Le Feu Sacre III, TOO FAT Lardies
Napoleonic Wargaming, Charles Grant with new material by C.S. Grant, Partizan Press, 2009
Napoleonic Wargaming For Fun, Paddy Griffith, History of Wargaming Project, has rules for both brigade and division level wargames that are suitable for Maida
Warmaster
Washington's Army in Peter Pig's Rules For the Common Man (RFCM) series could be adapted for Maida

Further Reading

Battle Tactics of Napoleon and His Enemies, Brent Nosworthy, Constable, 1995
Émigré and Foreign Troops in British Service (2) 1803-15, Rene Chartrand, Osprey Men At Arms
Forward into Battle: Fighting Tactics from Waterloo to the near Future, Paddy Griffith, The Crowood Press, 1990, in which Dr Griffith demonstrates that Oman's description of Maida, and his analysis of British infantry tactics in the Peninsular War, were mistakenly based upon firepower, rather than upon shock action with the bayonet.

History of the British Army Vol 5 Sir John Fortescue, Naval and Military Press reprint,
Maida 1806: Fifteen Minutes of Glory, Richard Hopton, Pen and Sword, 2002
Studies in the Napoleonic Wars, Sir Charles Oman, Napoleonic Library 6, Greenhill Books reprint, 1987, contains the original essay The Battle of Maida criticized by Paddy Griffith in *Forward into Battle* (above)
Tactics and the Experience of Battle in the Age of Napoleon, Rory Muir, Yale University Press, 1998

The historical battlefield map

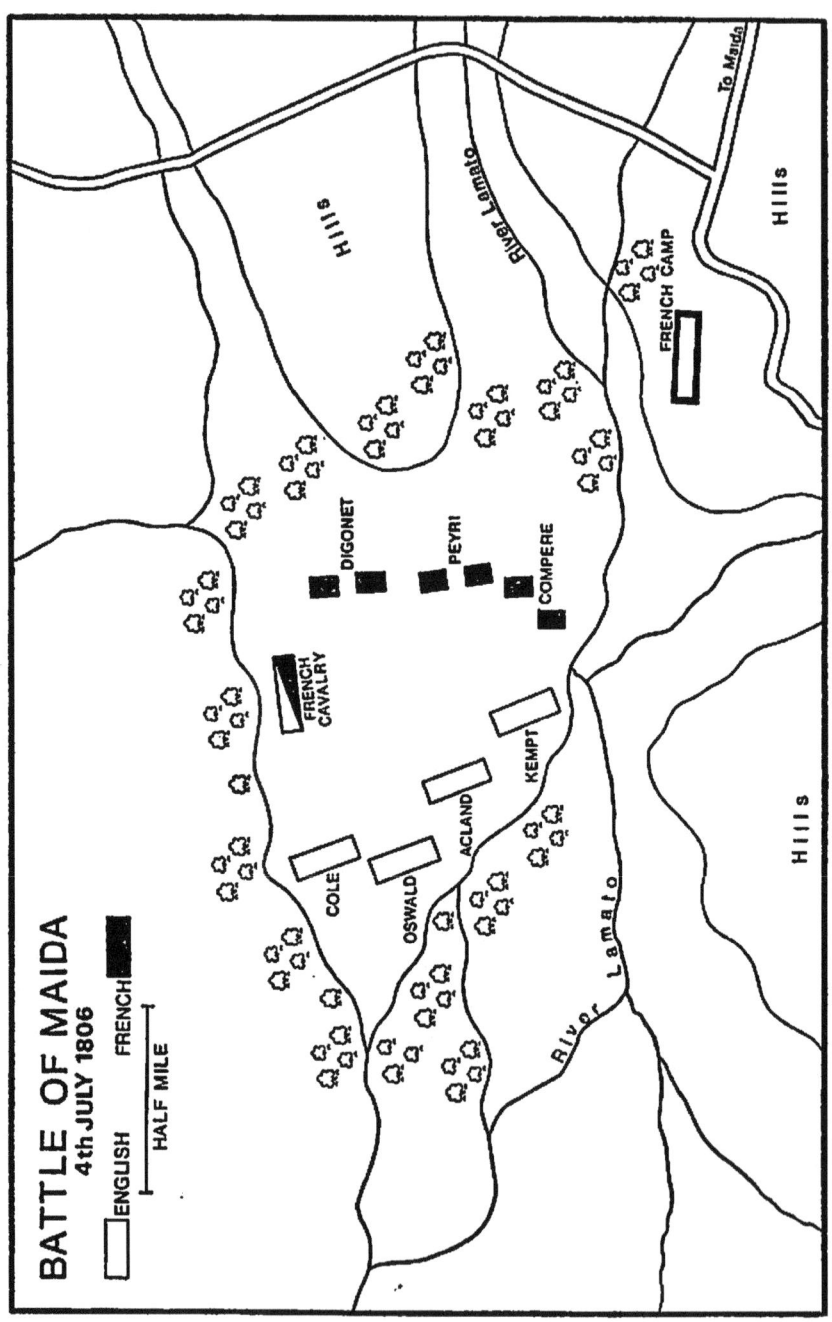

9. The Battle of Aliwal

28 January 1846

You are Sir Harry Smith[21], commanding the East India Company forces.

Historical Background
THIS WAS a brilliant action in which the powers of infantry, artillery and cavalry were successively and successfully brought into play, so that Sir John Fortescue, the historian of the British army, wrote '... it was the battle without a mistake'. As a Colonial horse-and-musket affair, this battle of the First Sikh War would be difficult to better.

Friendly Forces The Honourable East India Company's force, commanded by Sir Harry Smith, consisted of 10,000 infantry (two-thirds natives), 2,000 cavalry and 32 guns.

Enemy Forces The Sikh force, led by Ranjur Singh, had 18,000 infantry, 2,000 cavalry and 67 guns. The battlefield was a level grassy plain some two miles long and one mile wide, with the River Sutlej in the rear; at the edge of the plain was a gentle rise, between Bhundri on the Sikh right and the mud village of Aliwal, and the two villages were connected by waist-high earthworks, curving along the ridge and masked by a thin grove of trees. Holding both the villages, the Sikhs were positioned on the crest of the rising ground, their guns spaced along the front of their line, facing south-east; between the river and the ridge lay the tents of their encampment.

Construction of the terrain
It is necessary to bring the villages of Bhundri and Aliwal and the Sikh entrenchments nearer the river, with the fords positioned on the wargames table so as to form objectives. The River

The Sutlej can run right along the Sikh baseline to save it taking up valuable wargaming space. The terrain is completely flat, except where a low ridge runs right across the table between the villages. This can be formed by a table-length 'ridge' of books, wood, plastic tiles, etc, under a cloth.

---

[21] Sir Henry (Harry) George Wakelyn Smith, (born 28 June 1787) distinguished himself in the 95th Rifles in the Peninsular War. He was appointed Deputy-Adjutant-General of the forces in India, where he took part in the Gwalior campaign of 1843, for which he was appointed a KCB, and the Sikh War of 1845. He was in command of a division under Sir Hugh Gough at the battles of Mudki and Ferozeshah. After the latter action, Sir Harry Smith was appointed to an independent command.

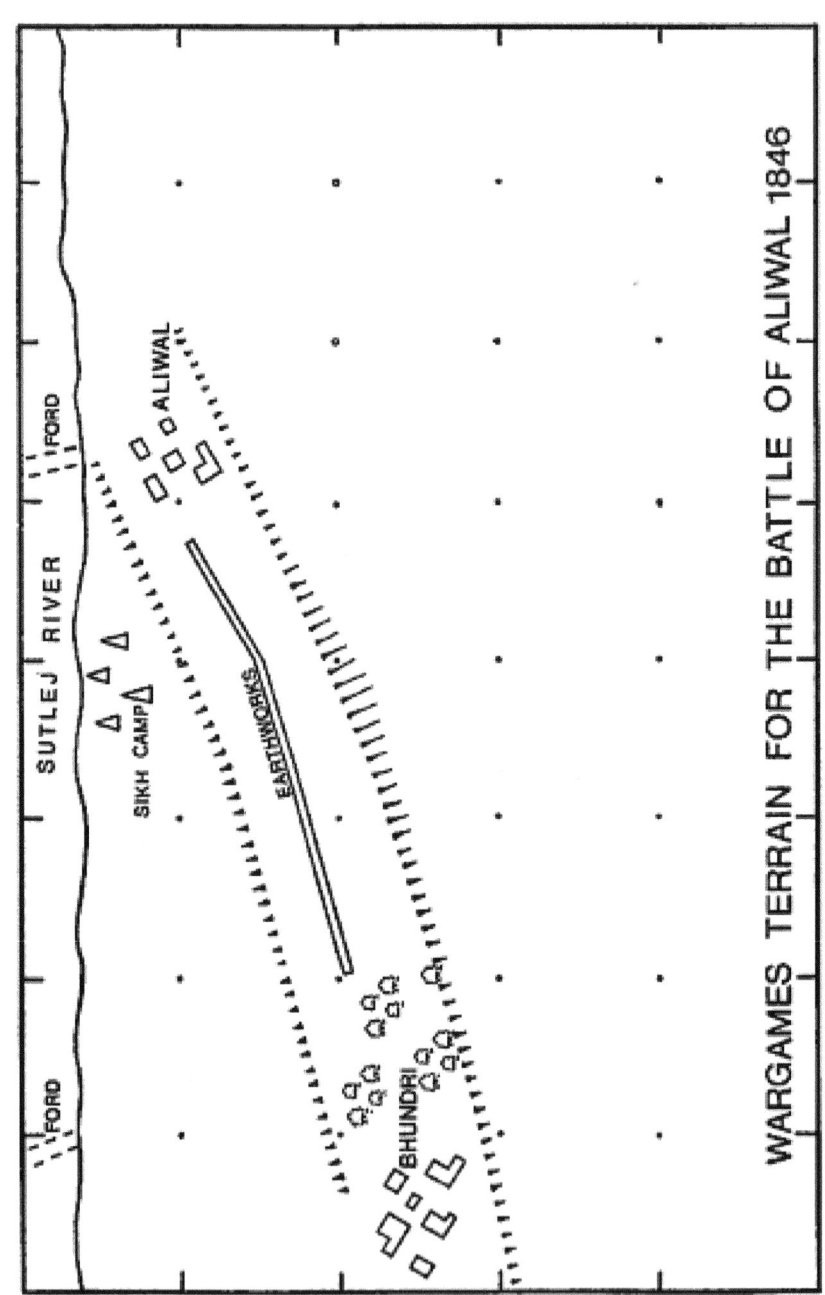

Stop! Read no further until you have deployed the forces and issued your detailed written orders.

The course of the actual historical battle.

At 10 am the British force began to move forward in an order of battle reminiscent of the Napoleonic Wars, each unit in line of column, the cavalry on the flanks and the artillery in the intervals. Commanded by veterans of the Peninsular War, the force's arms and equipment had not changed since Waterloo and, because of the northern Indian winter climate, the army wore the old-style European dress.

Sir Harry Smith intended to carry Aliwal first and then continue the attack upon the Sikh left and centre, cutting their line of retreat by the river fords. Under heavy artillery fire, the brigades of Godby and Hicks went forward towards Aliwal, taking a ragged volley at a hundred and fifty yards from the Irregular hillmen manning the position, who, lacking time to reload, were overwhelmed as the advancing infantry broke into the village, capturing two guns and killing all the gunners. Now a general attack was made upon the Sikh left and centre by Wheeler's Brigade, supported by Wilson; Wheeler advanced under heavy artillery fire, halting twice and lying down to steady the men and to allow Wilson's Brigade to draw level. When they were close to the Sikhs, the attackers fired a heavy volley, causing many enemy infantry to retreat, although the gunners continued firing their guns. Throughout, the Horse Artillery flashed in and out, pausing to fire, then limbering up and retreating out of range before being hit.

His left in serious danger of being turned, Ranjur Singh changed his front, pivoting on the village of Bhundri, and covering the movement with a large body of cavalry, who were immediately charged and routed by a Native Cavalry Regiment. Hicks' Infantry Brigade went forward to support the cavalry while Godby's Brigade hit the Sikh left flank and rear, carrying everything before them. With his retreat via the river fords seriously threatened, Ranjur Singh sent forward another large body of cavalry to cover him as he threw back his left and, using the village of Bhundri as a pivot, reformed his line at right-angles to the river.

A squadron of the 16th Lancers ordered forward to attack the Sikh horsemen sent them streaming away towards the river in full flight. Returning, this squadron broke through squares of crack Aieen Sikh infantry trained by French mercenary officers.

Wilson's Brigade went forward to attack an artillery battery still firing resolutely from the centre of the Sikh position, but took such heavy losses that the native battalions of the brigade began to waver. Brigadier Cureton ordered the 16th Lancers to support them by charging through the smoke and jumping the earthworks into the seven gun battery. Abandoning their guns, the Sikh artillerymen ran to the shelter of the squares formed by the Regular Sikh Infantry of Avitabile's Brigade, formed up behind the battery and supported by cavalry. The British horsemen broke through the squares, then turned back into their shattered ranks and the conflict broke up into small mêlées between Sikh infantry and cavalry and the 16th Lancers.

The battle was nearly over, the retreating Sikhs being rapidly followed up by Wheeler's and Wilson's Infantry Brigades. Bhundri, held by native irregulars, was stormed and captured by the 53rd Foot, which cleared out the enemy and captured many guns; the Sikh gunners resolutely stood their ground and fought to the death. Two batteries of Horse Artillery harassed the Sikh foot soldiers running in confusion towards the ford by their camp, where Ranjur Singh had nine pieces unlimbered to cover the ford; but these guns only fired once before they were overrun by the pursuers. The fugitives tried to escape across the river, losing stores, camp-baggage, supplies and all their 67 guns.

This is one of the most difficult battles to reconstruct realistically so that it culminates in the historical British victory. There are few sets of wargame rules that will allow an army to defeat a force almost twice its size, yet here the enemy is not only stronger in men and guns, but is also entrenched behind earthworks and in houses. The reconstruction must be slanted to balance these inequalities, so that the British can win; but the Sikhs must be given a chance of victory.

Outline of the enemy's orders.

Starting at the left flank, roll for which Sikh unit is positioned first, then roll to decide the next unit in the defensive line. The cavalry should be held in reserve and used to counter any British attempt to turn the flank.

Ratings of the Commanders and Military Possibilities
Sir Harry Smith showed himself to be an 'above average' commander, whereas his opponent, Ranjur Singh, displayed 'below average' ability; Cureton, the British cavalry commander, was also 'above average' and the Brigade commanders displayed exceptionally high qualities. It is extremely difficult for the British to 'destroy' the Sikh Army, as in a normal wargame, so the objective could be the Sikhs' need to maintain their lines of retreat over the two fords crossing the River Sutlej; thus the British commander will be required to manoeuvre so that he splits the Sikh force and herds it away from the vital river crossings. When the Sikh commander finds himself unable to prevent this, he will be forced to withdraw and concede the battle.

The Sikh force was surprised by the British advance, for it was marching out of its overnight encampment when Sir Harry Smith arrived on the horizon, and, lacking time to transport his entire army across the river to safety, Ranjur Singh had to send them back to man the earthworks they had thrown up on the previous night. To make the Sikh Army flow back in separate bodies, give their commander an 'order of march' away from his overnight camp, and mark on the map and on a Time Chart the progress of the first unit, then the second and so on, until the British force arrives (on the map). It is possible to ascertain the location of the Sikh units in relation to their defence works. On turning to man their position, the rearmost units will march back to Aliwal, each unit 'peeling-off' to conform to other units until they form a continuous defensive fine. Simultaneously, Sir Harry Smith is deploying his force into battle order far enough from the Sikh positions to take a minimum of artillery fire.

A successful reconstruction will depend upon local rules, together with the varying morale and fighting qualities of:

(a) European (British) infantry and cavalry,
(b) Native infantry and cavalry regiments of the British East India Company, officered by Europeans,
(c) Sikh Regular infantry and artillery, well trained on Western lines by European mercenary officers, and
(d) Irregular Native hillmen and cavalry.

The British-officered Native infantry regiments had been overawed by the martial Sikhs in previous battles, and this must show in their morale and fighting qualities. The Sikhs were brave, well trained and disciplined, and their artillerymen were prepared to stand by their guns to the death. A proportion of their army at Aliwal consisted of Irregular soldiers—battalions of hillmen and masses of irregular light cavalry—which were not particularly reliable when facing British troops. In mêlées all types of troops can be given a figure-valuation that varies according to the type of opponents they encounter. To these fighting figures must be added or subtracted other values—the morale of the attacker and defender; whether the attack is in flank, rear or downhill; whether the enemy are outnumbered or behind earthworks, etc. A suggested table is shown on preceding page.

Manipulation of morale status for varying types of troops is a most effective means of reconstructing any wargame between unequal numbers and types of forces. For example, native tribesmen under artillery fire or threat of cavalry attack must check their morale state, with prescribed penalties for these situations (which probably will adversely affect them). The resulting morale level may well cause them to move out of danger or even flee.

Horse Artillery galloping up to within close-range of the enemy, unlimbering, firing and then limbering up and retiring can be simulated on the wargames table by giving Horse Artillery in action the same move-distance as a Light Cavalry charge-move; then penalise them an eighth of their move-distance for the time it takes them to unlimber and another eighth to limber up. With a 24 inch move, therefore, a horse gun can limber up in its original firing position (3 inches) move forward 9 inches, unlimber (3 inches), fire, limber up (3 inches) and pull out a further 6 inches.

In simulating the cavalry actions of this battle it will be necessary to reproduce concealment through smoke and dust[22].

---

[22] See ideas for this in the chapter entitled Through Smoke and Dust- 'Now You See Them, Now You Don't' in *War Games Through the Ages Vol. 3 1792-1859*, Donald

Wargame Figures suitable for Aliwal

2mm

Irregular Miniatures Horse and Musket range has suitable close-order troops; irregular cavalry and elephants will be found in the Ancient range

6mm or 1/300 scale

Baccus has Napoleonic British troops.

Heroics and Ros have Napoleonic troops that could portray British and HEIC forces, whilst some figures from the Colonial range might pass muster as Sikhs.

Irregular Miniatures War in India range has Sikhs, HEIC sepoys and other suitable figures.

10/12mm

Old Glory UK Grand Scale has Napoleonic British troops, but no suitable figures for the Sikh forces.

Pendraken has Napoleonic troops, but nothing suitable for the Sikhs, save painting North-West Frontier Skh infantry in the appropriate colours.

15mm

Essex Miniatures has.

FreiKorp 15 has a Mahratta and Sikh Wars range.

Irregular Miniatures Renaissance to 18th century Moghul Indian/Persian range has many suitable figures; British Napoleonic troops can be used for Gough's army.

20mm

The website www.plasticsoldierreview.com/Index.aspx has no specific lists for this period, but suitable figures may be found elsewhere. Esci's Muslim Warriors, for example, listed under North-West Frontier (India) will make irregular Indian troops, whilst HaT's Colonial Wars Indian Infantry can be painted up as Sikh regulars. British and Company troops may be sourced from the Napoleonic or Crimean War ranges.

Irregular Miniatures have an Indian Mutiny range which contains many suitable figures; others can be found in the British Napoleonic range .

Featherstone, Stanley Paul & Co Ltd, 1975; see also Chapter 2, Surprise and Concealment, of *Advanced War Games*, and Chapter 14, The Viking Raid, of *War Game Campaigns*, both republished in the History of Wargaming Project.

25/28mm

Foundry Miniatures have suitable British troops in both shakos and caps and Sikh regulars. Other suitable figures may be found in the Indian Mutiny range.

Miniature Figurines does not have figures specifically for the Sikh War, but figures from the Colonial Indian and Indian Mutiny ranges might serve the purpose.

Old Glory has a Sikh War range, and some useful figures may also be found in the Indian Mutineers and Napoleonic British ranges.

Wargame Rules suitable for Aliwal

Black Powder: Battles with model soldiers in the age of the musket, Rick Priestley and Jervis Johnson, Warlord Games
The freewargamerules website has various sets of rules for the Colonial period; one could also use rules from the Napoleonic section for British, HEIC and Sikh regular troops.

Further Reading

Armies of the East India Company 1750-1850, Stuart Reid, Osprey Men At Arms 453
The British Army on Campaign (1) 1816-1853, Michael Barthorp, Osprey Men At Arms 193
The Sikh Army 1799 – 1849, Ian Heath, Osprey Men At Arms
Queen Victoria's Enemies (3) India, Ian Knight, Osprey Men at Arms 219
Queen Victoria's Commanders, Michael Barthorp, Osprey Elite 71

The historical battlefield map

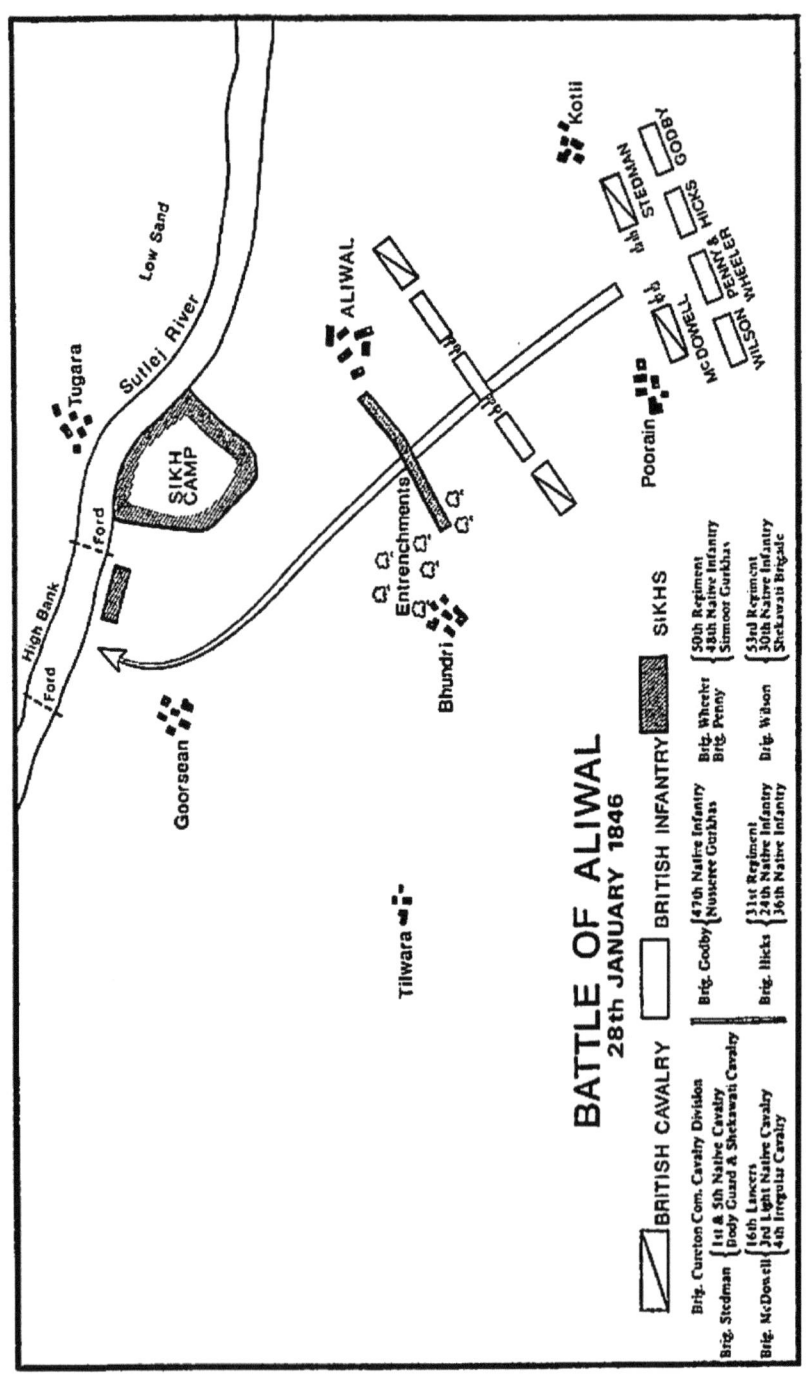

10. The Battle of Wilson's Creek

10 August 1861

You are General Nathaniel Lyon[23] of the Union Army.

Historical Background and forces

THE AMERICAN CIVIL WAR had just started, and General Nathaniel Lyon was fighting to keep the State of Missouri in the Union. The force raised by the Confederates outnumbered his, so Lyon hoped to strike a quick blow before the enemy had concentrated all their troops; realising that he had to retreat, he sought to counter the enemy superiority in cavalry, which made it difficult for him to disengage, by attacking their camp on Wilson's Creek, a meandering stream some ten miles from Springfield. Plans were made for the Union force to make a night march on 9th/10th August and attack the enemy from the north at dawn, while Colonel Sigel's flanking force, making a long detour by a side road, attacked from the south.

The Forces

The armies of both sides were similar in composition to those that had fought at Bull Run a few weeks earlier, with a few well disciplined and drilled Regular units, but mostly ill trained and badly disciplined volunteers.

Union Force Lyon's force of 4,282 men and 10 guns was made up of 2 small battalions of Regular infantry, 4 or 5 companies of Regular cavalry, 3 batteries of Regular artillery, 3 semi-Irregular Missouri Regiments (recruited from Germans in the St Louis area), 2 Volunteer Infantry Regiments from Kansas, and 1 Volunteer Infantry Regiment from Iowa.

Sigel's flanking force of 1,118 men and 6 guns consisted of 8 companies of the 3rd Missouri Volunteers, 9 companies of the 5th Missouri Volunteers and 2 companies of cavalry (121 troopers).

The Union forces are advancing from the top of the board towards the Confederate positions on the ridge either side of Wilson's Creek.

Sigel's flanking force should arrive south-west of Sharpe's house later in the battle.

---

[23] Nathaniel Lyon (born July 14, 1818) graduated from West Point in 1841 and served in the 2nd US Infantry in the Seminole and Mexican Wars, distinguishing himself in the Battle for Mexico City. He became a staunch Abolitionist and Republican while serving in the 'Bleeding Kansas' Border Wars. In January 1861, he wrote about the secession crisis, "It is no longer useful to appeal to reason, but to the sword."

Confederate Force Under General Ben McCulloch, the Confederate position was such that the sturdy Missouri State Guard, under Major-General Sterling Price, with its 5 brigades (commanded by Slack, Clark, Parsons, MacBride and Rains) was placed to receive Lyon's attack. On the bluffs east of Wilson's Creek were Hebert's 3rd Louisiana Regiment of infantry, well drilled and disciplined, and McIntosh's Arkansas Regiment. Further south were Pearce's 3 regiments of Arkansas Infantry with 2 batteries, while other troops under Greer, Churchill and Major were positioned along the valley. The force totalled 11,500 men, of whom perhaps 6,000 or 7,000 were in semi-fighting trim and participated in the battle. There were 15 guns.

In the area where most of the fighting took place, Wilson's Creek was fairly deep, with rough, steep and rather high banks, making fording difficult. On the left the hills were sheer like bluffs; on the right or western bank the ground was a succession of broken ridges, covered with trees and a stunted growth of scrub oaks with dense foliage, forming an almost impenetrable tangle in places. Rough ravines and deep gullies cut up the surface.

Construction of the terrain

It is necessary to compress the salient features of the field, and modify its undulations, vegetation and other topographical features so that it forms a practical battlefield for model soldiers to fight upon. The southern aspects (where Sigel attacked) must be brought nearer the area of the main battle line. Almost the entire right-hand third of the table forms a plateau steeply sloping down to the creek on the left and to the creek branch running off parallel to the cornfield; there must be a ravine with swampy ground immediately below Rain's camp. On the left of the table some irregular scrub-covered ridges will form the main area of fighting between Lyon and the Confederates. Further south, Skegg's Branch was bordered by fairly steep banks, with scrub-covered ground in the vicinity

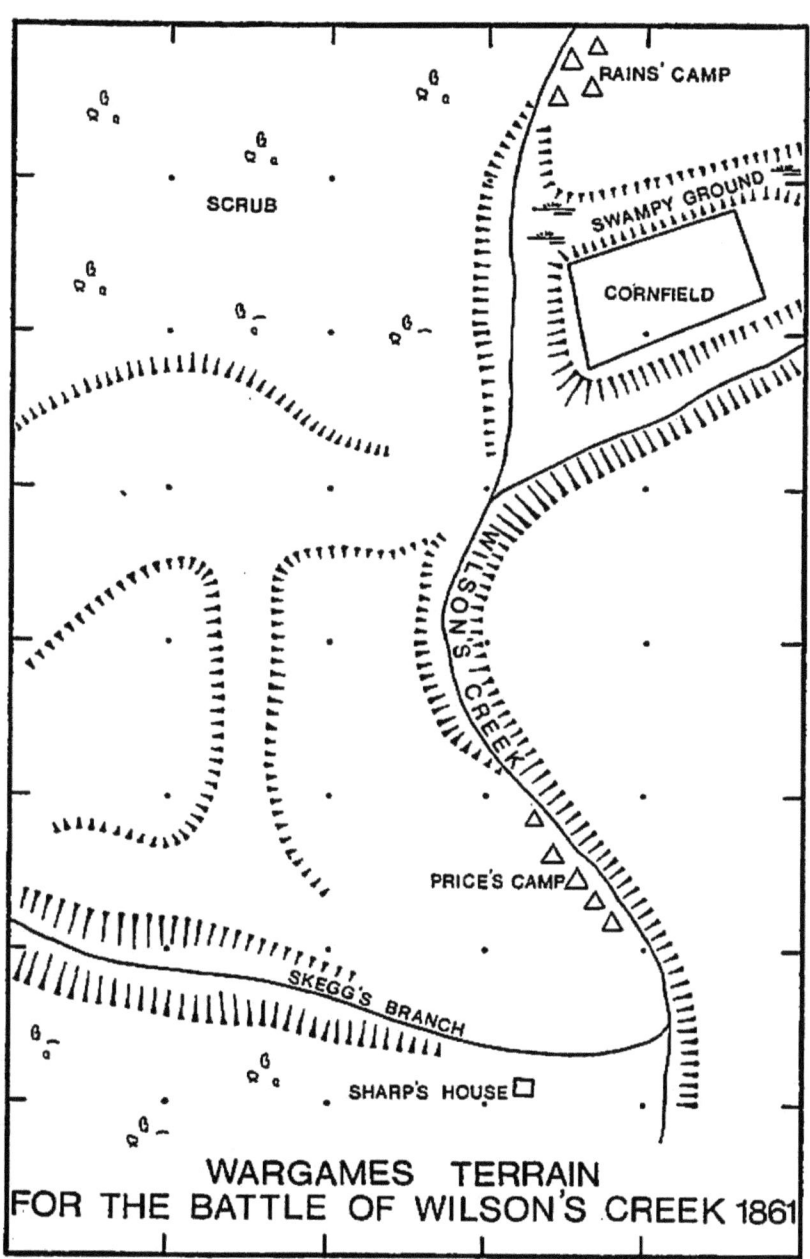

Stop! Read no further until you have deployed the forces and issued your detailed written orders.

The course of the actual historical battle.

Led by Plummer's battalion of Regular infantry, Lyon's force struck Rains' camp at 4 am, the escaping Confederates warning their main force of the impending attack. The Union force advanced one and a half miles until its skirmishers met the Confederate skirmish line and pushed them back to the ridge where the Confederates had formed their line. On the left Plummer became separated from the main body by a deep ravine and swampy ground; his men entered the cornfield which lay beyond to take on, and be checked by, a large force of the Louisiana Regiment. Then Dubois' battery disordered the Confederates in the cornfield, so that Plummer was able to draw off in good order. On the ridge both sides fought with great bravery and determination in ranks three or four deep at ranges of thirty to forty yards, with the muzzle-loaders doing great execution in an action that raged for more than an hour. Each side gave ground in turn, until at last the Confederates ceased coming forward, and a lull ensued.

At 5.30 am the sound of battle was briefly heard in the rear of the Confederates facing Lyon; then it died away, was renewed and finally ceased altogether. It was Sigel who, when he heard the firing from Lyon's action, had opened fire with his four guns, placed on the hill overlooking the enemy camp, then pushed his infantry across the Creek and entered the lower camp, the enemy fleeing before him as he advanced against slight resistance to Sharp's house, where the Union force formed line. McCulloch gathered a force and attacked them, to be mistaken by Sigel's men for friends, the confusion being intensified by the enfilading fire of Reid's battery east of the Creek. In the fight that followed Sigel's force was completely routed and by ten o'clock he was out of the fight.

Conscious that a third of his men were down, that Sigel's attack had failed and, while he had no reinforcements, the rebels in front of him seemed to have an unending supply of men, Lyon was heard to mutter: 'I fear the day is lost'. Then Lyon was killed leading an attack, and Major Samuel Sturgis assumed command. The death of their leader was not known to the Union troops, who fought manfully for the next hour in repelling repeated frontal attacks and attempts to turn their right flank. Both Union Regulars and Volunteers maintained their position against repeated Confederate charges. Despite the overwhelming numbers of Confederates on the field, the contest was evenly balanced until Dubois' Union battery moved up to pour a murderous fire into the enemy's right flank, making them recoil along their whole front. The Confederates drew off and the battle seemed to have ended.

At 11.30 am, informed of Sigel's rout, and conscious of his depleted and exhausted forces and a shortage of ammunition, Sturgis decided to withdraw to Springfield. Covered by artillery, he left the field, watched by the relieved Confederates, whose ammunition was exhausted, as were their men, who, lacking discipline, were unsuitable for the task of pursuing the Federals. As Dupuy says: 'Although this was a tactical victory for the South, Lyon's aggressive operations had saved Missouri for the Union.'

The losses for both sides were heavy:
Union, 223 killed, 721 wounded, 291 missing, totaling 1,234;
Confederate, 265 killed, 800 wounded, 30 missing, totaling 1,095.

Ideally, this reconstruction should be fought as two actions to allow for the possible effect of Sigel's attack on the main action, when the wargame map must be divided into the two areas of battle and each scaled up to fill a full-size wargames table. When Sigel is pressing forward into the Confederate position, or he has been turned back and his opponents return to fight off Lyon, the battle is transferred to a single table. If it is fought as one battle, Sigel's attack must be very carefully timed on the Time Chart; it will be moved on the map, to come on to the table 1½ hours after the main action has begun.

Outline of the enemy's orders.

The Confederates should be setup to maximise the defensive features of the ground, with a strong reserve arriving from the Price's camp. When the Union flanking force arrives, a strong force should be dispatched to deal with it.

Ratings of the Commanders and Military Possibilities

Lyon is 'above average', McCulloch and Price 'average' and Sigel 'below average'.

Lyon's high rating helps to balance the Confederate numerical superiority, as will the varying fighting qualities and morale of Regulars and Militia, with the latter showing variable and widely fluctuating standards in both aspects. Although the Confederates seemingly had about 11,500 men, apparently only some 6-7,000 took part in the battle. Therefore the remainder must be occupied elsewhere, posted in outlying villages and areas, and a Military Possibility can bring them either marching to the scene of the action (on the map at scaled move-rate) or cause them to remain where they are for fear of being attacked. The former Possibility would provide an alternative objective, in that Lyon has to defeat the Confederates facing him before the arrival of reinforcements.

The morale of the Regulars should enable them to remain steady while their Militia comrades, although being given the chance to display the same courage, are liable to give way under stress. The factors governing firing and hand-to-hand fighting must be loaded in the Regulars' favour, to simulate the steadiness under fire that results from discipline and training.

At the onset of the battle the Confederates fleeing from Rains' camp warned the main force of the impending attack, though the sound of firing would have had the same result—a Military Possibility could consist of a strong wind blowing away from the camp and carrying away the sound of firing (see chapter called 'Weather in Wargames' in *Advanced Wargames).* The Time Chart must show the time of the attack on Rains' camp, delay for possible resistance, the time (measured in distance) taken by the escaping soldiers to reach the main camp, and the delay while the alarmed soldiers are roused and commanders issue their orders. Meanwhile, Lyon's force is steadily advancing.

Surprise and confusion will undoubtedly cause the Confederates to form up hastily, since few were well trained or disciplined soldiers. This initial advantage for Lyon's smaller force can be simulated by allotting a specific period of time for the Confederates to form up and move forward to the battle line; the shorter this period, the less prepared is the battle line, with a subsequent depreciation in its fighting ability and morale.

The scaled-down armies of wargames' tables reduce the ranks from three or four to two deep, but, even so, double-rank firing will be extremely effective. A marked feature of the American Civil War[24] was regiments running from the firing line, to be rallied a hundred yards back and to return and fight bravely. Hence, the battle line in this encounter will show units dropping out, moving up to fill gaps, and being outflanked; and it will test the stoutheartedness of their commander in most realistic fashion.

A Military Possibility might arise from the sound of Sigel's attack in their rear affecting the morale of the troops holding off Lyon's force. This could be represented by Chance Cards or a personal morale-check on individual commanders such as McCulloch and Price, or even unit commanders.

In the early morning mist and smoke, Sigel's men mistook oncoming Confederates for friends. This situation is probably best handled by the wargamer representing Sigel drawing a Chance Card, which might bear an instruction such as 'Hold fire until oncoming troops within 6 inches as they may be friends' or other injunctions, ranging from the best from his point of view to the worst. Plummer's regiment on the Federal left could take advantage of a Military Possibility to act differently, although it seems that, together with Dubois' battery, his force held the attention of a much larger group of Confederates than itself.

Lyon's death was kept from his army, but a Military Possibility might make nearby units aware of it. The small Federal army was primarily held together by the strong personality and enthusiasm of Lyon, so that his death could have an adverse effect upon its morale—this must be reflected if necessary. Historically, Lyon's successor Sturgis, almost out of ammunition, drew off what was left of his exhausted force and

---

[24] For analyses of American Civil War tactics and troops' behaviour in battle, see *Rally Once Again: Battle Tactics of the American Civil War* by Paddy Griffith, The Crowood Press, 1987; and *The Bloody Crucible of Courage: Fighting Methods and Combat Experience of the American Civil War*, by Brent Nosworthy, Constable, 2005.

withdrew to Springfield. Thus, the ability of the Federal force to withdraw from the field in good order (providing they have administered proportionately equal casualties to the Confederates) should provide them with some satisfaction, though the tactical victory will go to the South. Perhaps more than any other of our battles, this one is likely to satisfy both commanders.

Figures suitable for Wilson's Creek

2mm

Irregular Miniatures have Horse and Musket models which could be painted as American Civil war armies.

6mm or 1/300 scale

Adler Miniatures has an American Civil War range.

Baccus has an American Civil War range.

Heroics and Ros have an American Civil War range.

Irregular Miniatures have an American Civil War range.

10/12mm

Irregular Miniatures (have an American Civil War range.

Magister Militum has an American Civil War range.

Miniature Figurines, now owned by Caliver Books of Nottingham, has an American Civil War range.

Old Glory UK Grand Scale has an American Civil War range.

Pendraken has an American Civil War range.

15mm

Essex Miniatures has an American Civil War range.

FreiKorp 15 has an American Civil War range.

Irregular Miniatures (www.irregularminiatures.co.uk) have an American Civil War range.

Miniature Figurines have American Civil War troops.

Peter Pig has an extensive American Civil War range.

20mm

Many wargamers began their tabletop campaigning with the Airfix Union and Confederate infantry sets, though their depiction of the troops' equipment was far from accurate!
The website www.plasticsoldierreview.com/Index.aspx lists a large number of sets by several manufacturers for the American Civil War, and the IMEX Mexican-American War US Infantry might also be used to portray soldiers wearing the peaked forage cap still sometimes worn by Confederate units.

Irregular Miniatures have an American Civil war range.

25/28mm

Essex Miniatures has an American Civil War range.

Foundry Miniatures have an extensive American Civil War range.

Irregular Miniatures have an American Civil war range.

Miniature Figurines has an American Civil War range.

Old Glory has an American Civil war range.

Perry Miniatures has an American Civil War range.

Wargame Rules suitable for Wilson's Creek

Black Powder: Battles with model soldiers in the age of the musket, Rick Priestley and Jervis Johnson, Warlord Games
Civil War Battles, Peter Pig Rules For the Common Man
The freewargamerules website has a whole section devoted to rules for the American Civil War
The Junior General website has simple rules in a Battle of First Bull Run (1861) scenario that could be used to fight Wilson's Creek.
Polemos: American Civil War – On They Came, Baccus 6mm
They Couldn't Hit an Elephant, TOO FAT Lardies

Further Reading

American Civil War Armies (1) Confederate Troops, Philip Katcher, Osprey Men At Arms 170
American Civil War Armies (2) Union Troops, Philip Katcher, Osprey Men At Arms 177
American Civil War Armies (4) State Troops, Philip Katcher, Osprey Men At Arms 190
American Civil War Armies (5) Volunteer Militia, Philip Katcher, Osprey Men At Arms 207
American Civil War Artillery 1861-65 (1) Field Artillery, Philip Katcher, New Vanguard 38
American Civil War Commanders (3) Union Leaders in the West, Philip Katcher, Osprey Elite 89
American Civil War Commanders (4) Confederate Leaders in the West, Philip Katcher, Osprey Elite 94
The American Civil War (2) The War in the West 1861- July 1863, Stephen Engle, Osprey Essential History 10
Bloody Hill: The Civil War Battle of Wilson's Creek, William R. Brooksher, Brassey's Inc, 1995

The Confederate Army 1861-65 (3) Louisiana & Texas, Ron Field, Osprey Men At Arms 430
The Confederate Army 1861-65 (4) Virginia & Arkansas, Ron Field, Osprey Men At Arms 435
The Confederate Army 1861-65 (6) Missouri, Kentucky & Maryland, Ron Field, Osprey Men At Arms 446
Confederate Artilleryman 1861-65, Philip Katcher, Osprey Warrior 34
Confederate Cavalryman 1861-65, Philip Katcher, Osprey Warrior 54
Confederate Infantryman 1861-65, Ian Drury, Osprey Warrior 6
Flags of the American Civil War (1) Confederate, Philip Katcher, Osprey Men At Arms 252
Flags of the American Civil War (2) Union, Philip Katcher, Osprey Men At Arms 258
Flags of the American Civil War (3) State & Volunteer, Philip Katcher, Osprey Men At Arms 265
Union Cavalryman 1861-65, Philip Katcher, Osprey Warrior 13
Union Infantryman 1861-65, John Langellier, Osprey Warrior 31

The historical battlefield map

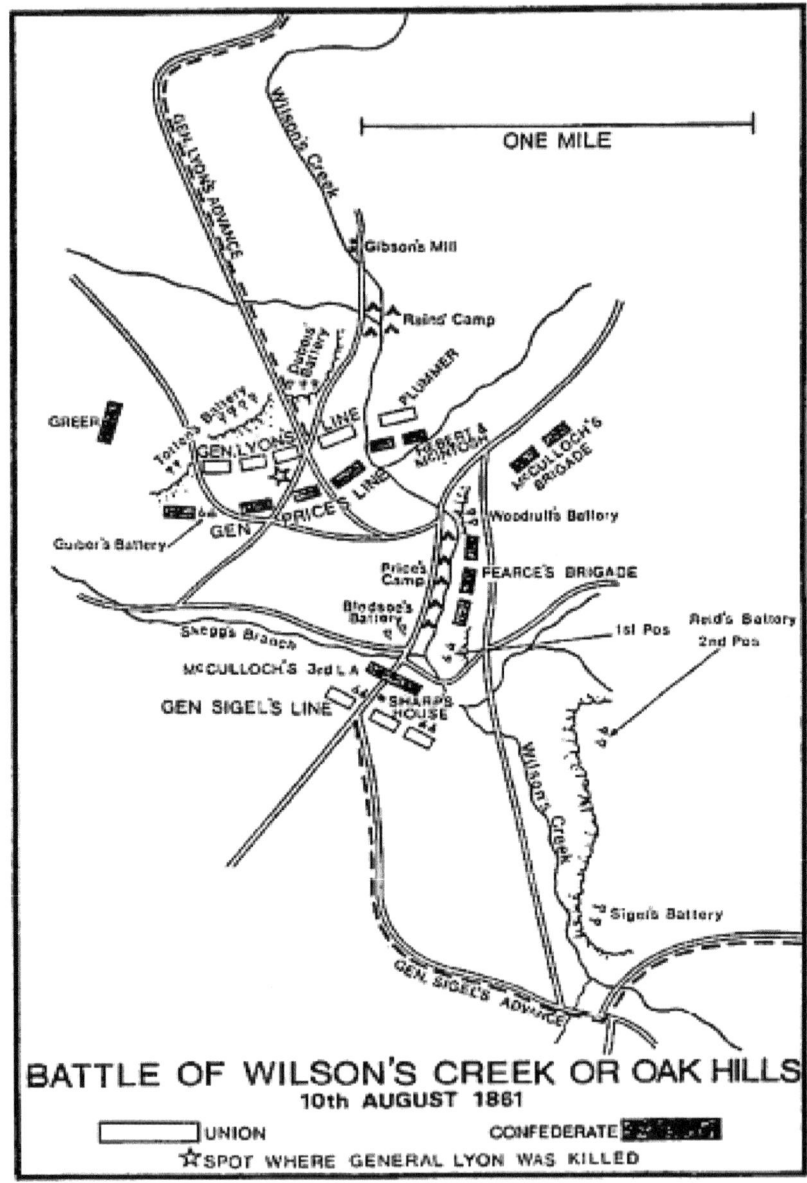

11. The Battle of the Little Big Horn[25]

25 June 1876

You are Lieutenant-Colonel George Armstrong Custer, hero of the Civil War[26] and famed Indian fighter. You realize this campaign is probably the last chance for anyone to achieve fame in the Indian wars.

Historical Background

ONE OF the last battles in which the American Indians resisted the white man, this consisted of two entirely separate actions. First, Major Reno's troops in the valley, retreating before an overwhelming force of Indians, were joined by Captain Benteen's force, and defended themselves on the bluffs across the river until late on the following day. In the other action, fought nearly five miles away, five troops of the 7th Cavalry under George Armstrong Custer were overwhelmed and wiped out in less than an hour by a large Indian force.

U.S Cavalry Forces

Lt-Colonel George A. Custer took his 7th Cavalry, consisting of about 600 soldiers, 44 Indian scouts and 20 guides, in pursuit of a large Indian force, with the idea of compelling them to fight to avoid being trapped between converging columns. On sighting the Indians, Custer impetuously decided to attack them, without realising that the Indian force consisted of about 5,000 warriors, the majority Sioux and Cheyenne under Crazy Horse, Sitting Bull and Gall.

Historical U.S. Cavalry Plan

At about noon on 25 June Custer divided his command into three battalions—Companies A, G and M under Major Marcus A. Reno; H, D

---

[25] See the Wikipedia entry for the battle for further information
http://en.wikipedia.org/wiki/Battle_of_the_Little_Bighorn

[26] Custer (born 5th December 1839) was admitted to West Point in 1858, but graduated last in his class. However, on the outbreak of the Civil War, all potential officers were needed, and he was called to serve with the Union Army.

He fought from the First Battle of Bull Run to the Appomattox campaign. His association with several important officers helped his career, as did his performance as an aggressive commander. Custer was promoted to the temporary (brevet) rank of Major-General – hence he is often popularly called 'General Custer' - but at the end of the war reverted to his permanent rank of Lieutenant Colonel.

After the Civil War, Custer was dispatched to the West to fight in the Indian Wars.

and K under Captain Frederick W. Benteen; and C, E, F, I and L under his own immediate command; with B Company protecting the pack train, which was to follow the main column as closely as possible. Benteen scouted left of the trail while Custer and Reno proceeded along opposite banks of a small creek towards the Little Big Horn valley. Reno, with 112 men and 20 scouts, was told to cross the river and attack a camp on the west bank, while Custer turned right to support him in the river bottom by suddenly appearing at the lower end of the Indian camp and attacking its flank and rear.

Indian Forces

Lakota, Northern Cheyenne and Arapaho, led by Crazy Horse and Gall. Sitting Bull was more of a religious inspiration for the Indian tribes rather than a war leader.
The number of Indians may have been 1,800, giving a ratio of 3:1 against Custer.

Construction of the terrain
The battle is best fought along the length of the table, with the scene of Reno's action at the bottom, where the lower eighth of the table is raised to form a plateau with steep slopes descending to the river. A series of scrub-covered ridges and valleys will form the top half of the table, representing the ground on which Custer fought. It is not a difficult terrain to make, and the ridges and hills can either be formed of set piece features or by moulding a cloth over shapes beneath it.

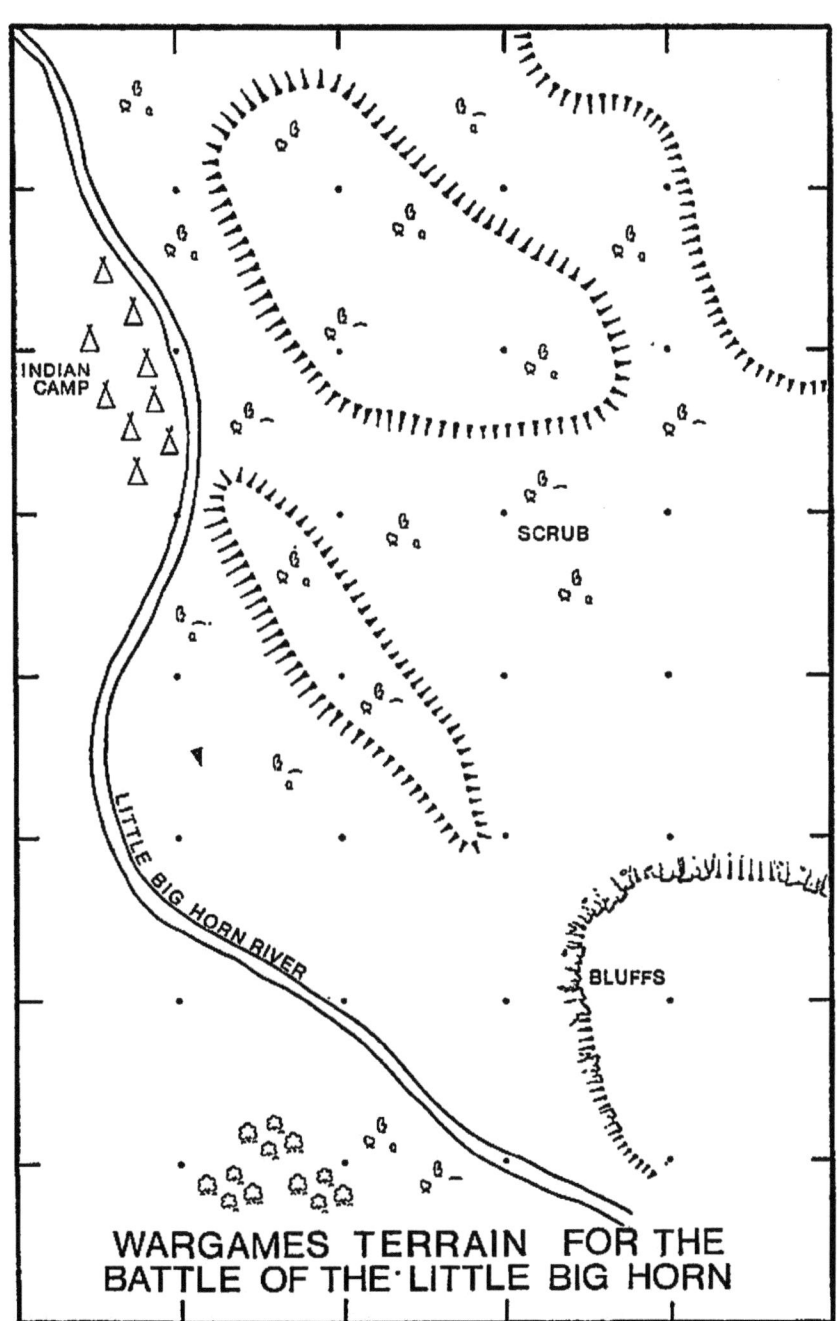

Stop! Read no further until you have deployed the forces and issued your detailed written orders.

The course of the actual historical battle.

So, at 2.30 pm Reno crossed to the west of the Little Big Horn River and advanced down the valley towards the Indian camp, but soon he was attacked by hordes of Indian warriors. His men dismounted and deployed in a skirmishing line, fighting on foot for half an hour, until the increasing numbers of Indians forced them to make a defensive stand in a timber thicket. Reno ordered his men to mount and retreat to the bluffs, a move which became a panicky flight as the Indians attacked the soldiers crossing the river, where they lost three officers and forty men killed, wounded or seeking cover in the brush. Across the river, on the east side, the survivors took up a defensive position on the top of a hill, but the Indians did not follow.

Leaving Reno, the mass of Indians started after Custer's column, which had advanced to the junction of two ravines just below a spring, where Custer dismounted two companies, under Keogh and Calhoun, to fight on a knoll. The remaining three mounted companies continued along the ridge and then dismounted to occupy a line, about three quarters of a mile long, along the first considerable ridge beyond the river.

Gall and his warriors were the first to engage Custer, before another large party under Crazy Horse moved from the lower part of the encampment up a ridge to cut Custer off from the village. Outnumbering Custer's men by as many as 20 to 1, the Indians did not rush madly to the attack, but fought on foot and from prone positions, as did the Americans. Large numbers of Indians wriggled along gullies and hid behind knolls all round the troops—it was a terrain that lent itself to this style of fighting. Many of the troopers' horses were shot to make breastworks, but only 225 cavalrymen, their ammunition running out, could not hold out against as many as 5,000 warriors. The action is believed to have lasted about an hour, and it is said to have ended when the Indians stampeded the soldiers' horses, so that they lost the extra ammunition in their saddle-bags. This was immediately followed by a concerted Indian attack, so successfully and swiftly carried out that within minutes not an American trooper remained alive. There was no final charge on horseback as portrayed in writings and paintings.

Just after three o'clock Benteen and his three companies pushed forward and joined forces with Reno's depleted and shaken command in defensive positions on the high bluffs. An hour later, Captain McDougall came up with his company and the train of pack mules.

Believing that Custer might need assistance, Captain Weir took Company D, followed by Benteen and the other two companies of his battalion, to a point about one and a half miles to the north-east, when large numbers of Indians began a frantic ride to cut them off. In a few minutes the force was so threatened that the troopers dismounted and prepared to fight on foot. Realising that the position from which they had set out was the stronger, and to make the force a more compact body, Weir ordered a withdrawal, and no sooner had the force reached its original position on the bluffs than Indians appeared from everywhere and heavy firing was exchanged until dark, when the warriors withdrew to the valley. During the night the troopers dug trenches and made barricades of food boxes.

The Indians resumed the attack at dawn and fighting continued throughout the morning and afternoon, when the warriors withdrew, leaving a small group to harass the cavalrymen. Late in the afternoon the Indians fired the grass in the valley to cover the departure of the entire Indian encampment. During the two days of fighting, Reno and Benteen lost 32 men killed and 44 wounded. Indian losses in the entire action have never been precisely known, but published figures vary from 30 to 300.

As Custer's and Reno's battles were well separated, this is another reconstruction that lends itself to being fought as two actions, each bearing upon the other in the long run. The only other choice is to telescope them together and, with wargamer's licence, fight them on the same table at the same time, modifying the reconstruction by:
   (a) telescoping the two fields of action,
   (b) having Custer try to rejoin Reno, on realising the odds against him, and
   (c) allowing the Indians to split to fight Custer and Reno, with the latter's defensive position drawing off enough Indians to give Custer a chance.

In fact, the attack on Reno ceased when the Indians started after Custer's column, which more or less rules out the only, though remote, chance of reversing the decision. Historically, when Custer's men were slain, the Indians returned to attack Reno; in a table-top simulation, only if and when either Custer or Reno are wiped out, will the Indians concentrate on the remaining force, so that both actions occur simultaneously.

Custer's initial objective was to destroy the Indians and their encampment, but his advance turned into a fight for survival, giving rise to an alternative objective — that if Custer and Reno put up a prolonged resistance, the Indians should be allowed a given percentage of losses or a time limit and, when either of these is reached, the Indians will have to withdraw.

Outline of the enemy's orders.

Indian tactics often looked somewhat random to the U.S. Cavalry, but Custer noted in his book, *My Life on the Plains*[27] that any threat to their women and children (in their village) would draw the braves to battle. Thus roll a single die for each group of braves:
1, 2 or 3 they remain stationary (and may fire),

---

[27] Published two years before his death. A modern paperback edition was published by Applewood Books in 2009 and may be obtained from www.amazon.co.uk

4 or 5 they move towards the nearest Cavalry and halt and fire when within 12 inches,
6 they attempt to charge.
Crazy Horse was a key commander in the battle. Therefore any Indian band he is with may alter the die score by 1.

Ratings of the Commanders and Military Possibilities

Custer rates 'below average' and the Indian chiefs 'average'. This reconstruction presents a peculiar problem: if the heavily outnumbered 7th Cavalry is to have *any* chance of success (if not the reconstruction becomes purely historical), strong factors must give the Americans parity with the Indians. This is difficult, because the Indians were as good as if not better fighters in this environment than the Americans; and their morale was certainly as good, probably higher. Thus, the usual 'differing morale' method of handling numerical inequalities cannot prevail here, and disparity in numbers must be tackled through the firepower of the 7th Cavalry when opposed to the relatively poor trade muskets and even bows and arrows of the Indians. The .45-70 Springfield carbine, carried by troopers in addition to their Colt revolvers, fired a hard hitting bullet with a flat trajectory, and had a much greater range than any weapons carried by the Indians. Reflect this by allowing the cavalrymen greater range and the ability to fire much more frequently (perhaps three times per game-move), though rapid fire causes them to run out of ammunition quickly.

An alternative method of handling the numerical disparity, though this method precludes an accurate reconstruction, is to precede the actual game by a period of map-moving, giving Custer the opportunity of manoeuvring advantageously so as to use his superior firepower against Indian groups in detail rather than *en masse*.

A Military Possibility can be introduced to prevent Custer's horses being stampeded along with the reserve ammunition. If so, the possibility of the Americans running out of ammunition during the course of the battle, due to the rapid expenditure of the cavalry carbine, should be reflected in subsequent events.

Reno's party is said to have scrambled back across the river in confusion, which, in a wargame, will have to be put down to low morale; and on reaching the bluffs they will have to be rallied. If they do not rally, they will flee the field, taking with them all the realism of the reconstruction. If they are not considered to have been routed, their hasty withdrawal has to be tacitly accepted as part of the wargames action, and some 'local' rules devised to cover it.

A Time Chart can be a great help when reconstructing this action, tying in the various movements of Custer, Reno, Benteen, Weir and the Indians.

Figures suitable for the Little Big Horn

2mm

Irregular Miniatures have Horse and Musket troops which could be painted as US Cavalry; Indians would have to be represented by suitable models from the Ancient range.

6mm or 1/300 scale

Heroics and Ros have suitable US cavalry figures in the American Civil War range, but no Plains Indians.

Irregular Miniatures have a Plains Wars range with Indian and 7th Cavalry.figures.

10/12mm

Irregular Miniatures (have a Plains Indians range; suitable US troops can be found in the American Civil War range.

Miniature Figurines, now owned by Caliver Books of Nottingham has American Civil War cavalry, but no Plains Indians.

Old Glory UK Grand Scale has an American Civil War range, but no Plains Indians.

Pendraken's nineteenth century range includes the Plains Wars.

15mm

Essex Miniatures has suitable cavalry figures in the American Civil War range but no Indians.

FreiKorp 15 has a Yellow Ribbon Indian Wars range.

Irregular Miniatures American Indian range includes both Plains Indians and US Cavalry figures.

Miniature Figurines has Plains Indians and Cavalry in the Wild West range; other suitable figures may be found in the American Civil War range.

Peter Pig has ranges of US Cavalry and Plains Indians.

20mm

Airfix made US Cavalry, 'Red Indians' (no political correctness back then!) and Wagon Train sets; the latter could be used to provide wagons, sutlers, and Indian agents.

The website www.plasticsoldierreview.com/Index.aspx has an American Western Frontier section, which lists many military sets, including several for Custer and the 7th Cavalry, others for civilians and their Native American opponents.

Irregular Miniatures have a Plains Wars range.

25/28mm

Foundry Miniatures have US Cavalry, Plains Indians and other suitable figures in their Old West range.

Irregular Miniatures have suitable US Cavalry figures in the American Civil War range, but the only Indians in the Characters of the Wild West range are on foot...

Wargame Rules suitable for Little Big Horn

Black Powder: Battles with model soldiers in the age of the musket, Rick Priestley and Jervis Johnson, Warlord Games
The freewargamerules website has a set of rules entitled *Counting Coup on Custer: Fast Play Rules for the Little Big Horn Battle* in the 19th Century section.
Hey you in the Jail! covers the small battles that were common in the West, Peter Pig Rules For the Common Man
The Junior General website has a Battle of Little Bighorn scenario and simple rules.

Further Reading

A Terrible Glory: Custer and the Little Bighorn – the Last Great Battle of the American West, James Donovan, Grand Central Publishing, 2009
Little Big Horn 1876: Custer's Last Stand, Peter Panzeri, Osprey Campaign 39
The American Indian Wars 1860-1890, Philip Katcher, Osprey Men At Arms 63
The Last Stand: Custer, Sitting Bull, and the Battle of Little Big Horn, Nathaniel Philbrick, Bodley Head, 2010
The Plains Wars 1757-1900, Charles M. Robinson III, Osprey Essential History 59
Red Sabbath: The Battle of Little Bighorn, Robert Kershaw, Ian Allan Ltd., 2008
Son of the Morning Star: General Custer and the Battle of Little Bighorn, Evan S. Connell, Pimlico, 2005
Tribes of the Sioux Nation, Michael G. Johnson, Osprey Men At Arms 344
US Army Frontier Scouts 1840-1921, Ron Field, Osprey Elite 91
US Army in the Plains Indian Wars 1865-1891, Clayton Chun, Osprey Battle Orders 5
US Cavalry on the Plains 1850-90, Philip Katcher, Osprey Men At Arms, 168
US Cavalryman 1865-1890, Martin Pegler, Osprey Warrior 4
Warriors at the Little Big Horn 1876, Richard Hook, Osprey Men At Arms 408

The historical battlefield map

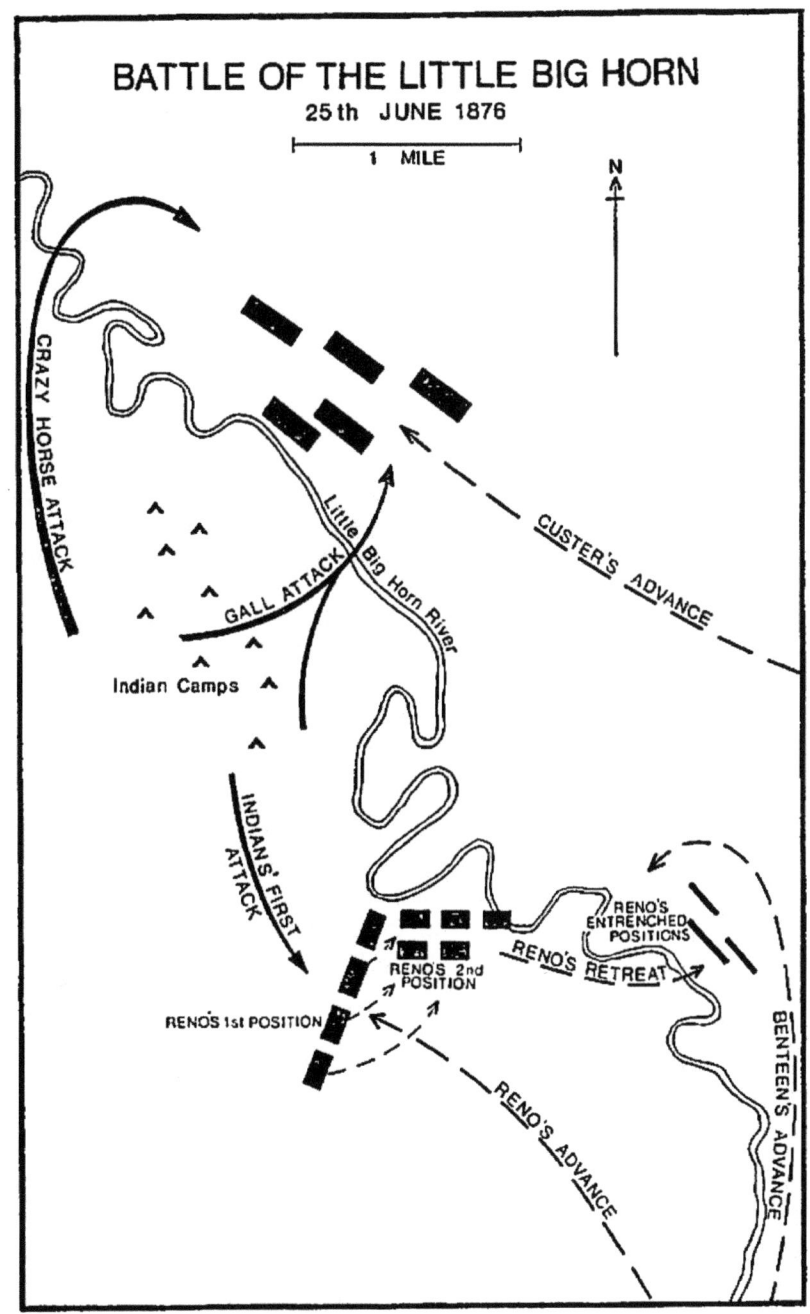

12. The Battle of Modder River

28 November 1899

You are Lord Paul Methuen[28], commander of the 1st Division.

Historical Background

THIS BATTLE was fought during the Second Boer War between the British 1st Division, commanded by General Lord Methuen, and Transvaal and Orange Free State Boer commandos under Generals Cronje and De La Rey.

Methuen's column, moving to the relief of Kimberley, had to cross the Modder River, which, like many South African rivers, ran through a miniature canyon about thirty feet below the level of the veld, where a long line of bushes and trees marked its east to west course. Methuen had no map of the area nor any details of the surrounding country, and discounted information about a weakly held drift lower down the river. He did not expect much opposition, as he was convinced that only about 400 Boers had been left behind to delay his force.

Anticipating the usual British frontal attack, the Boers had constructed elaborate defences: entrenchments masked by shrubs and brushwood stretched for five miles along both banks giving Boers on the southern bank a clear field of fire across the coverless veld, which sloped gently towards them. Their smokeless powder offered no visible target, so that the British artillery would almost certainly range on buildings on the north bank, where seven field guns were positioned. There was also a heavy gun (probably a 100-pdr) on high ground to the rear. Numerous artillery emplacements were constructed to delude the British into thinking they had silenced the guns when they had, in fact, been moved from one place to another. Whitewashed stones placed on the veld gave exact ranges both to the Boer gunners and

---

[28] Paul Methuen, 3rd Baron Methuen, was educated at Eton, served two years in the Royal Wiltshire Yeomanry and joined the Scots Guards in 1864. He was promoted to captain in 1867 and was appointed adjutant of the 1st battalion in 1868.

He served in the Ashanti campaign of 1873 - 1874 on the staff of Sir Garnet Wolseley, was promoted to Lieutenant-General in 1876. He was the commandant of headquarters in Egypt for three months in 1882, being present at the Battle of Tel el-Kebir.

He served in Sir Charles Warren's the expedition to Bechuanaland in 1884 to 1885, where he commanded a corps of mounted rifles. He was deputy adjutant-general, in South Africa from 1888. He was promoted to Major-General in May 1888. He served in 1897 as press censor at headquarters on the Tirah expedition and was promoted to Lieutenant-General in 1898. He was then given the command of the 1st Division on the outbreak of theWar in South Africa.

riflemen. On the Tewee Rivier, a tongue of land between the Riet and the Modder, they dug-in a 'pom-pom' and two field guns, and they also positioned several Maxims and machine guns along their front.

In short lengths, the trenches were irregularly aligned, with their parapets concealed by rocks and bushes. Each held about six men. The farmhouses and buildings were converted into strongpoints. The Transvaalers were on the left of the position while the Orange Free Staters were on the right; it is thought that De La Rey positioned the latter with their backs to the river so that they would find it harder to break off the fight than they had done in their previous two battles.

Friendly Forces 8,000 British and Empire forces

> British Naval Brigade
> 9th Lancers.
> Royal Horse Artillery with 12 pounders
> Royal Field Artillery: 18th, 62nd and 65th Batteries with 15 pounders
> Royal Engineers
> 3rd Grenadier Guards.
> 1st and 2nd Coldstream Guards.
> 1st Scots Guards.
> 1st Northumberland Fusiliers:
> 2nd Black Watch
> 2nd Northamptonshire Regiment:
> 1st Loyal North Lancashire Regiment:
> 2nd Yorkshire Light Infantry
> 1st Highland Light Infantry
> 2nd Seaforth Highlanders
> 1st Argyll and Sutherland Highlanders
> Army Service Corps.
> Army Medical Corps.
> Kimberley Light Horse
> Diamond Fields Horse
> Australian Troops.
> Colonial Mounted Irregulars
> Rimington's Scouts.
> South African Reserve.

Enemy Forces 9,000 Boers.

Their guns are concentrated around the hospital and to the north of the bridge.

Construction of the terrain

The Modder River will bisect the width of the board just above its centre, thus allowing ample space for the Boer positions in front of the river and for the British main area of action. There must be adequate space on the British left flank for the attack on the farm and the subsequent crossing of the river by the dam, and also sufficient on the right flank in case a Military Possibility allows the Coldstream Guards to cross at the shallow point. The ground above the river should be slightly raised, so that the Boers have a field of fire over the heads of their men in the trenches forward of the river. The heavy gun can either fire from the hill at the top left-hand corner of the table or 'off the table' as a 'map-shoot'.

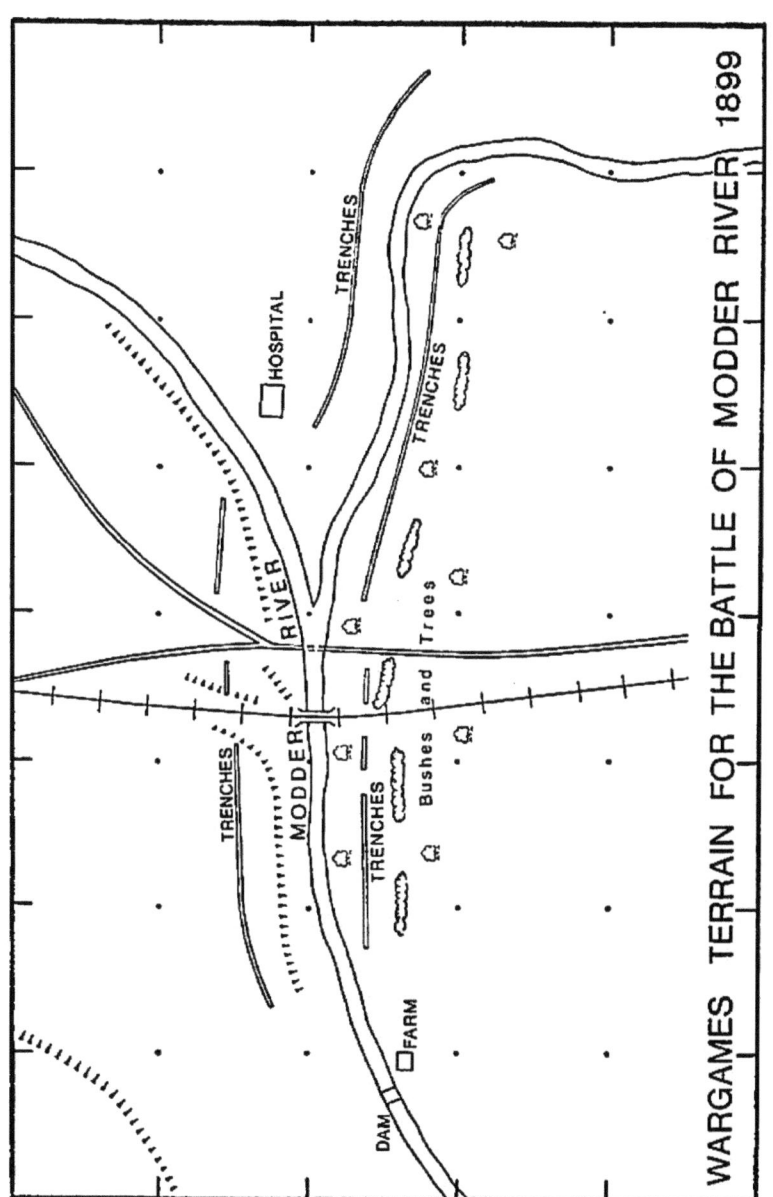

Stop! Read no further until you have deployed the forces and issued your detailed written orders.

The course of the actual historical battle.

About 6.30 am the British 18th and 75th Field Batteries unlimbered on the right and opened fire at a range of 4,500 yd. Boer guns replied with a flash and a faint film of blue-white smoke instantly dissolving in the air. This long-range firing continued for some time, until the Boer guns ceased firing to give the impression that they had been silenced, and that their small rearguard was falling back. At that time the 9th Lancers, patrolling about a mile from the river, withdrew under a sharp fire to the extreme right of the line, where they took no further part in the battle.

At the regulation five paces interval, the Guards moved majestically down the slope, Scots Guards on the right, 3rd Grenadiers and 2nd Coldstream echeloned to the left, and 1st Coldstream in the rear. Descending the smooth grassy slope leading gently down to the river, they got to within 800 yd of the enemy's trenches when suddenly from along the whole extent of the Boer front came musketry interspersed with Maxim fire. The advancing British fell flat to the ground, to be pinned down under a pitiless sun for the remainder of the day, their slightest movement attracting a storm of bullets.

The 1st Coldstream Guards, extending to the right to cover and support the Scots Guards, found to their surprise that they were halted by the Riet River running south to north, a fact completely unknown to the mapless Methuen. Nor was he aware that a few hundred yards back was Bosnian's Drift, where a crossing could have been made in strength, taking the entire Boer position on the Modder in reverse. A small party of the Coldstream Guards managed to cross the river, but at a place that was obviously impossible for large numbers of men. The battalion dug themselves in so that the entire Brigade of Guards were out of the battle, and it was not yet 8 am. With the halting of the attack, the artillery, in positions less than 1,300 yd from the Boer trenches, spent the day covering the north bank with shrapnel.

Far away to the left the 9th Brigade pressed forward, Northumberland Fusiliers on the right, King's Own Yorkshire Light Infantry in the centre, North Lancashires on the left, and the Argyll and Sutherland Highlanders in support of the right and centre. The KOYLI and Lancashires stormed a farmhouse in a kraal just to the south of the dam, getting within charging distance of the buildings by moving along an unseen and unprotected shallow ditch running down to a small clump of trees by the river bank. The Boers in the farm and in the trenches on either side were unable to fire on them for fear of hitting each other. Recklessly leading an attempt to cross the river, Lord Methuen himself was wounded and compelled to hand over his command to Brigadier Colville. Led by General Pole-Carew, the KOYLI, one by one, clambered across the river on the dam under a heavy fire, until 400 men had formed up on the other side; then they pushed along the north bank hoping to take the enemy in flank. Unfortunately, they were mistaken for Boers and fired upon by their own artillery, which compelled them to fall back. However, their appearance on the north bank so alarmed the lukewarm Orange Free Staters that at 2 pm, a large number of them mounted and rode off; at 4 pm there was something resembling a general stampede as the Boers retired along the deep river bed out of sight of the British, who did not realise what was occurring.

Earlier in the afternoon the 62nd Battery, after dashing sixty two miles in twenty eight hours, arrived and immediately went into action, together with the rest of the artillery, as the centre of the battle moved towards the left of the position. An attempt to resume the Guards Brigade attack failed in the face of heavy fire, so it was decided that they should move out under cover of darkness, cross the river to the left and storm the enemy position.

In the early evening, after eight hours of continual fighting, the remainder of the enemy retreated, unknown to the British, leaving behind their guns and many of their wounded. Later that night they mustered up courage to return and collect them. The British bivouacked on the field where they had fought and next morning made an unopposed crossing of the river to take the abandoned enemy position.

British casualties were 466 men killed, 20 officers and 393 men wounded, and the Boers lost 60 killed and 300 wounded, in what was a military farewell to the nineteenth century, in that the bewildered British soldier found himself severely punished through being tactically untrained to tackle a dug-in enemy possessing a high rate of firepower.

As the Boers have numerical parity with the British, plus superb cover, how can the British enter this battle with even the slightest chance of success? Here is a selection of Military Possibilities that might affect the course and eventual result of the action:

1. The OFS commandos are given a lower morale standard than their Transvaal comrades so that, under stress, they break and retire.
2. The British force can discover the existence of Bosnian's Drift lower down the Modder River and cross there, turning the Boer flank. However, while this move may provide an interesting wargame, it takes all reality from the battle.
3. Pole-Carew's success on the left flank can be exploited.
4. The Coldstreams' abortive crossing on the right could be made a successful venture, again turning the Boer position.
5. The Boers' (particularly the Free Staters') lack of experience and dislike of being on the receiving end of artillery fire can be reflected by morale penalties when under fire, so that they might break at any point, particularly when the heavy guns of the 62nd Battery arrive.
6. The Boers' defensive dispositions were all made in anticipation of a British frontal attack, and De La Rey had early nervous moments when the Guards moved towards the flank before veering centrewards. A flank attack would have caused De La Rey to alter his dispositions completely, under artillery fire, or else withdraw. Again, however, this detracts from the realistic reconstruction of the battle.

Outline of the enemy's orders.

The Boers maintain a static position, although individual units change their fire positions. They will retire if threatened with outflanking.

Ratings of the Commanders and Military Possibilities

De La Rey stood out in comparison with the other leaders but to make him an 'above average' commander and Cronje 'average' is to overweigh the Boers' already strong hand. Therefore, both De La Rey and Cronje should be rated as 'average', and Methuen 'below average', but Pole-Carew, on the British left, could be rated as 'average'. Or it might be more realistic to rate De La Rey and Pole-Carew as 'above average', and Cronje and Methuen 'average'.

In spite of their inability to move forward, the British Regular soldiers cannot be considered to be low in morale or in fighting ability, if only because they possessed training and discipline superior to that of the Boers. The penalty for a low morale rating for the British soldier could be for them to 'go to ground' when they come under heavy Boer fire, when they have three choices:

1. Once down they take no casualties but cannot fire back.

2. Remaining on the ground, they can return fire but take half casualties.

3. They can fire on their feet and move their full distance, or they can move and fire with half effect, or they can charge-move and make contact with the entrenched Boers.

The condition governing each choice rests upon their state of morale under fire, decided by throwing a die for each group and deducting 1 from it (a) for *any* losses, (b) if they come under fire from a group of men approximately twice their strength, (c) if they arc under artillery fire, or (d) if they are under fire from flank or rear.

To be able to rise to their feet and move or fire, a group needs to total 3; to stay down and return fire the group needs to total 2; to stay down without casualties and without returning fire is their normal basic reaction, and is what they will do if unable to make the required totals.

The Transvaalers' morale will benefit from being behind cover but they should be rated as equal in morale and fighting ability to the British Regulars in fire-fights but slightly lower in mêlées because of their fear of the bayonet. Having shown a disinclination to fight at the earlier battles of Graspan and Belmont, the Orange Free Staters are regarded with some contempt by the Transvaalers, and it might be a reasonable Military Possibility to insert a built-in distrust in the game rules so that their actions are not well coordinated. The lower quality of the Free State Troops should be reflected in their morale and fighting ability.

Having received a grim lesson from British Lancers at Elandslaagte, the Boers greatly feared the lance, yet the 9th Lancers played no part in the Battle of Modder River. A Military Possibility could permit them to move from the right flank if desired.

The British artillery's firing on its own men on the left can be controlled by Chance Cards or, as the firing will be 'off-table' map-shooting, a certain allowance can be accepted for inaccuracy of aim. If it should happen that the Biritsh soldiers are hit, their morale must immediately be checked, with a 'distraction' factor to allow for their being fired on by their own side.

One realistic way of refighting this battle is to give the wargamer representing Methuen only the details that were known to the British commander in 1899 — 400 Boers forming a rearguard - only to discover, as did Methuen, that the situation is very different. As Methuen had no map of the area and discounted local information, the wargamer playing Methuen must be told that some or all of the information may be false; he has no alternative, therefore, but to make his plans and dispositions on a sketch-map conforming to his own vague idea of the terrain and what he is told that he can see. (This must be done *before* he sees the table-top terrain.) The Boers will mark their dispositions on their own accurate map, and the troops from each side will be shown when action demands. Any casualties caused by artillery fire will be deducted on paper, the map being marked accordingly by the Boer commander, and morale checked whenever necessary. He will move on paper as if on the actual table, but any men breaking cover (such as in rout or in changing their position) will have to be revealed on the table.

The battle might, in fact, be fought in two parts, as the British front was three miles long, and the soldiers at one end had no idea what was happening at the other.

Figures suitable for Modder River

2mm

Irregular Miniatures Horse and Musket or generic modern troops could be used.

6mm or 1/300 scale

Heroics and Ros have Colonial British troops, but no Boers, though perhaps some American Civil War figures might pass muster appropriately painted.

Irregular Miniatures have British troops and Boers in their Colonial range.

10/12mm

Pendraken has a Boer War range; other suitable figures may be found in the North-West Frontier range.

15mm

Essex Miniatures has Colonial British troops but no Boers; there may be suitable figures in the American Civil War range.

Irregular Miniatures have British troops and Boers in their Colonial range.

Miniature Figurines has British troops for 1899-1902 and Boers in the Crimea to the Trenches Colonial Wars range.

20mm

Airfix never made colonial period British infantry or Boers, so ingenious wargamers cut the spikes off the WWI German Infantry's pickelhaubes and painted them as sun helmets! The Cowboy and Wagon Train sets provided suitable figures for the Boers.

The website www.plasticsoldierreview.com/Index.aspx lists six Strelets sets in its Second Anglo-Boer War section; other suitable British infantry may be found in its North-West Frontier (India) section, while the GerMan Cuban War Spanish Infantry might also double as Boers.

25/28mm

Essex Miniatures Colonial range only covers the Sudan campaigns.

Foundry Miniatures have suitable British troops in the Colonial range, but no Boers.

Irregular Miniatures have British figures for the Sudan and Mahdist campaigns in their Colonial range, but no Boers.

Miniature Figurines has British troops in its Colonial Wars, and Boers in its South African, ranges.

Old Glory has a Boer War range.

Perry Miniatures has very a small Mafeking 1900 range which might be used with their Sudan range for British troops.

Wargame Rules suitable for Modder River

Black Powder: Battles with model soldiers in the age of the musket, Rick Priestley and Jervis Johnson, Warlord Games
The freewargamerules website has numerous sets of rules for the Colonial period.

Further Reading

Boer Commando 1876-1902, Ian Knight, Osprey Warrior 86
The Boer War 1899-1902, Gregory Freemont-Barnes, Osprey Essential History 52
The Boer War, Christopher Wilkinson-Latham, Osprey Men At Arms 62
The Boer Wars (2) 1898-1902, Ian Knight, Osprey Men At Arms 303
The British Army on Campaign (4) 1882-1902, Michael Barthorp, Osprey Men At Arms 201
Lord Methuen and the British Army: Failure and Redemption in South Africa, Stephen M. Miller, Routledge, 1999
More Military Blunders, Geoffrey Regan, Carlton Books Ltd., 2004
Queen Victoria's Enemies (1) Southern Africa, Ian Knight, Osprey Men At Arms 212

The historical battlefield map

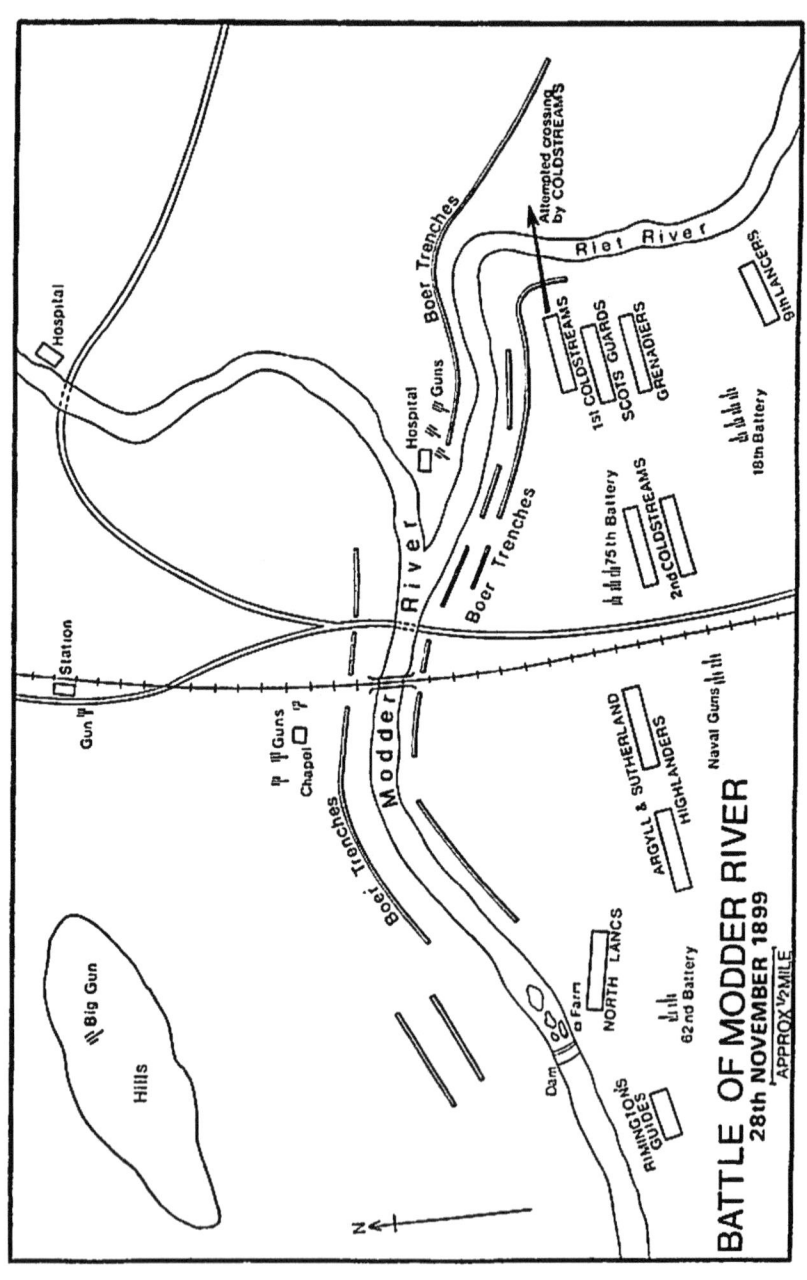

13. The ANZAC Landing at Gallipoli

25 April 1915

You are The ANZAC[29] force on the first day of the Gallipoli landings.

Historical Background

AT DAWN FORTY EIGHT small boats crept towards the shore at Ari Burnu; a flare shot up, a warning was shouted and sporadic fire broke out as about 4,000 men of the 1st Australian Division landed in three successive waves on a two thousand yard front. As the men grouped on the beach in the steadily improving light of day, it became obvious that the landing had taken place on the wrong beach -the soldiers had been told they would find a low sandbank, whereas this beach was backed by almost sheer shrub-covered cliffs.

Nevertheless, since it had been drilled into the men that everything depended on moving quickly inland, the Australian soldiers scrambled up the steep slope to a small flat area— subsequently known as Plugge's Plateau—just in time to see Turkish soldiers hastily disappearing down precipitous slopes into a vast scrub-covered ravine, later to be named Shrapnel Valley.

Friendly Forces
The first troops to land were two companies of each of the 9th, 10th and 11th Battalions of the Australian 3rd Brigade. The companies embarked from three *Formidable*-class battleships; HMS *Queen*, HMS *London* and HMS *Prince of Wales*. Each battleship dispatched four steamboats towing three row boats (launches and pinnaces)—a total of 48 boats. The table top battle starts shortly after the chaotic landing.

Around 10am reinforcements enter the table from the newly arrived 1st Brigade; one company from the 1st Battalion and two from the 2nd Battalion.

Enemy Forces
A battalion of 700 Turkish infantry supported by off-table artillery.

Construction of the terrain
This is hard yet easy—only a sand table or moulded plasticine[30] can adequately reproduce the ruggedness of the area yet, because it was so irregular, almost any formation is suitable, providing the named salient features are represented. Moulding a cloth over 'hills' will

---

[29] Australia and New Zealand Army Corps

[30] Trade name of a modelling clay manufactured by William Harbutt; sometimes used as a generic term for any modelling clay that does not set.

suffice, providing that the slopes, except where known to be precipitous, are climbable by model soldiers. The whole terrain can be littered with small pebbles, gravel, etc. (In fact, dog-biscuit fragments, when scattered around, give a terrain a remarkable resemblance to rocky ground.) Use lichen moss to represent the profuse thickets, but remember that the model troops have to be able to stand up; the natural features should serve as obstacles to channel troops away from the control of their commander.

One of the few certain occurrences during the action was the destruction of the mountain gun battery on Plateau 400. For the sake of accuracy, this battery should be placed on Plateau 400 and remain there for a designated number of moves, when the battery commander can, by a die throw, Chance Cards, etc, decide whether or not circumstances dictate a move before he is wiped out. The Turkish artillery that destroyed him will be firing 'off-table' on a 'map-shoot', but the mountain battery is permitted to fire at whatever enemy it can see on the table.

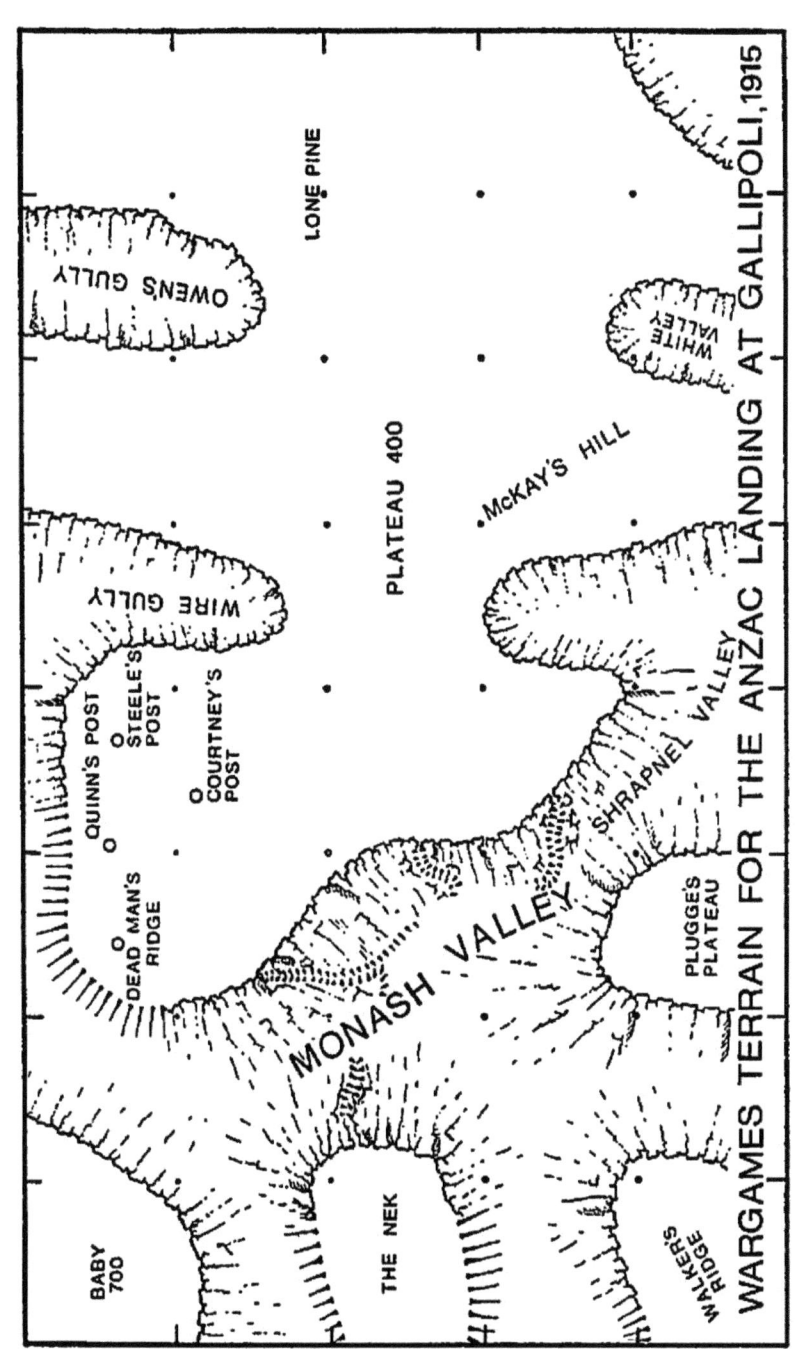

Stop! Read no further until you have deployed the forces and issued your detailed written orders.

The course of the actual historical battle.

In spite of the general confusion caused by the difficult ground and intermixing of units, by 6 am about 4,000 Anzacs were ashore and moving rapidly inland, driving the 700 or so Turks in the area back in disorder towards Baby 700 and Mortar Ridge. By 7 am small detached parties of Australians and New Zealanders had crossed Legge Valley, and the capture of all objectives seemed imminent. But, as the sun climbed high in the clear sky, the battle increased in intensity, with Turkish resistance mounting.

New arrivals splashing ashore at Anzac Cove were sent to Shrapnel Valley to reform and be despatched to various parts of the confused battlefield. Maps were useless and orders based on them could not be carried out: some New Zealanders took over an hour to move from Plugge's Plateau to Russell's Top because the map did not show an impassable 'razor edge' between them; six guns of an Indian Mountain Battery were, with incredible effort, dragged on to an exposed position on Plateau 400, where Turkish artillery soon wiped them out. The brief firing of this battery was the only artillery support the infantry received throughout the day, as the Navy lying offshore could not fire for fear of hitting their own troops. By 2 pm more than 12,000 Anzacs were ashore, opposed by about 4,000 Turks, but numbers were a dubious advantage, as the nature of the ground, the confusion caused by landing in the wrong place, and the intermixing of units blunted their striking power.

The ground was very difficult to fight on—covered with arbutus, dwarf holly, oak and stunted pine between three and twelve feet high and so thick in places as to be impassable. The scrub-covered rocky sides of Monash Valley were steep and precipitous; at this time of the year it was an arid valley with no exit save the almost perpendicular waterfalls that scored its sides. The most important, and bitter, fighting raged around the narrow ridge— a hundred yards wide and with a sheer drop on both sides—which connected Plateau 400 with Baby 700 and The Nek. A party of Australians had occupied The Nek by 8 am, a group under Captain Lalor remaining there while Captain Tulloch took the rest of the men over to Baby 700.

Mustapha Kemal, the best of the Turkish commanders, was in charge in this area and, bringing his troops up quickly, he forced Tulloch's small party to the back slopes of Baby 700, the Turks establishing themselves on its Western slopes and infiltrating its seaward flanks, so that it was not long before the Anzacs were forced to regroup just above The Nek.

At 11 am two companies arrived to reinforce them and, joining with Lalor's men, they charged the summit of Baby 700 and occupied the position. This summit changed hands no less than five times, as the local numerical superiority of the Turks drove the Australians from it and then, as reinforcements rushed up from

Anzac Cove, they in their turn drove the Turks back. But by 3 pm the Australian and New Zealand troops, reduced to the fragments of seven battalions all intermixed and without their familiar officers, were fighting with increasing desperation for the vital high ground above Monash Valley.

Between 4.30 and 5 pm a Turkish counterattack, developing across Legge Valley to Plateau 400 and down the slopes of Baby 700, drove the remaining Anzacs back into positions on either side of Monash Valley and The Nek. Captain Lalor was dead and reinforcements ceased to arrive. The Turks came on in waves, suffering very heavy losses but fighting bravely; neither side took any prisoners and groups of men were cut off and killed to a man in the frenzied and savage conflict.

At dusk the Anzacs were clinging to a series of detached positions at the end of Russell's Top, along the eastern side of Monash Valley and just inland of the crest of Plateau 400. A party of New Zealanders hung on to a vital position just south of the abandoned Nek. Colonel Pope occupied the small rocky eminence at the head of Monash Valley, subsequently known as Pope's Hill and, to his right along the eastern crest of the valley, detachments of men were clinging to exposed positions, subsequently known as Quinn's, Courtney's and Steele's Posts; to the south the Anzacs had been driven almost to the seaward edge of Plateau 400. By 5 pm the Anzacs, fighting for their lives, were being driven back to the sea, with everyone praying for night to fall. In the event, they held on.

Essentially, this will be a wargame fought between small groups of men completely separated from each other by steep hills and precipitous scrub-covered valleys. The success or otherwise of one group will have little immediate effect upon others fighting in the next valley or on the next plateau. Like Pork Chop Hill, this action is a jumbled affair fought desperately between small detached parties of men. It is best to set up a terrain and, with Anzacs and Turks in their right numerical proportion, let the battle fight itself. The objectives are for the Anzacs to hold on and for the Turks to throw them back into the sea. The Anzacs, to win the battle, must hold all or most of those positions they were holding at nightfall on 25 April 1915—at the end of Russell's Top; on the eastern side of Monash Valley; just inland of the crest of Plateau 400; just south of The Nek; Pope's Hill, the small rocky eminence at the head of Monash Valley; the exposed positions subsequently known as Quinn's, Courtney's and Steele's Posts; and the seaward edge of Plateau 400. Each could be allocated a points value, and an agreed total has to be reached for the Anzacs to win.

Outline of the enemy's orders.

The Turkish 57th Regiment led by Mustafa Kemal will counterattack from the left hand side of the table. Mustafa issued his famous order, "I do not expect you to attack, I order you to die! In the time which passes until we die, other troops and commanders can take your place!" The 1st battalion will attack against towards Baby 700. The 2nd battalion will arrive between 'Baby' and 'The Neck'. More troops attack from the left hand side of the board.

Ratings of the Commanders and Military Possibilities

As any general commander can exercise little or no influence on this muddled action, the Anzacs can be led by Captains Lalor and Tulloch, although they only represent two out of dozens of officers present. The local effect of Mustapha Kemal must be reflected by an 'above average' classification.

Morale must be calculated for each individual group. Throughout the morale of the Australian and New Zealand troops was first-class. At the beginning the Turkish troops' morale was poor, but, under the influence of Mustapha Kemal and buoyed up by local successes, it should rise on a sort of sliding scale. For the first third of the game Turkish morale could be low, for the second third normal, and for the final third as high as that of the Anzacs; or it can begin at 'average', rising and falling in accordance with local successes.

The battle can either begin with the Anzac groups in position, as far forward as Baby 700, and then fighting grimly to hold their positions while being pushed back by increasing groups of Turks, who arrive at specified times; or with the Anzacs moving from the beaches across the terrain towards the features they historically reached, the movements of both sides being coordinated on Time Charts. One method of simulating the inaccurate maps and general confusion is to have the Anzac force controlled by an outside commander, who will be given a deliberately faulty map and prevented from seeing the table-top terrain; he will receive vague messages from the troops fighting forward of him and will order the reinforcing troops forward from Anzac Cove by sending written instructions to their commanders but, as his map is inaccurate, those commanders may well be bewildered by his instructions, and the troops will probably fail to arrive at the places at which they are most desperately needed.

Figures suitable for the ANZAC landing

2mm

Irregular Miniatures generic modern troops could be used.

6mm or 1/300 scale

Irregular Miniatures have ANZAC troops in the World War I Colonial range, and Turkish troops in the main listing.

10/12mm

Pendraken has an ANZAC pack listed separately, but Australian and Turkish troops are listed under Middle East.

15mm

Irregular Miniatures have Turks in their Balkan Wars range, but no ANZAC's in their British range for World War I.

Miniature Figurines has British and ANZAC troops in its Crimea to the Trenches World War one range.

20mm

Airfix only made British and German infantry for the early war period.

The website www.plasticsoldierreview.com/Index.aspx has extensive lists of figures under World War I: ANZAC troops are listed under Commonwealth and Turkish troops under Ottoman.

Irregular Miniatures have Turks but no ANZAC troops in their World War I range.

25/28mm

Foundry Miniatures have Australian Infantry, but no Turks, in the Great War range..

Irregular Miniatures have Turks listed separately, and ANZAC troops in the Colonial section of their World War I range.

Wargame Rules suitable for Gallipoli
The freewargamerules website has numerous sets of rules for First World War trench warfare, which could be adapted to fight Gallipoli.
If the Lord Spares Us, TOO FAT Lardies

Further Reading
The Agony of Gallipoli, John Laffin, The History Press, 2005
Gallipoli, L. A. Carlyon, Bantam, 2003
Gallipoli 1915: Frontal assault on Turkey, Philip Haythornthwaite, Osprey Campaign 8
Gallipoli 1915, Tim Travers, NPI Media Group, 2004
Gallipoli: The Turkish Story, Kevin Fewster, Allen & Unwin, 2003
Ottoman Infantryman 1914-1918, David Nicolle, Osprey Warrior 145
The Australian Army at War 1899-1975, John Laffin, Osprey Men At Arms 123
The Ottoman Army 1914-18, David Nicolle, Osprey Men At Arms 269

The historical battlefield map

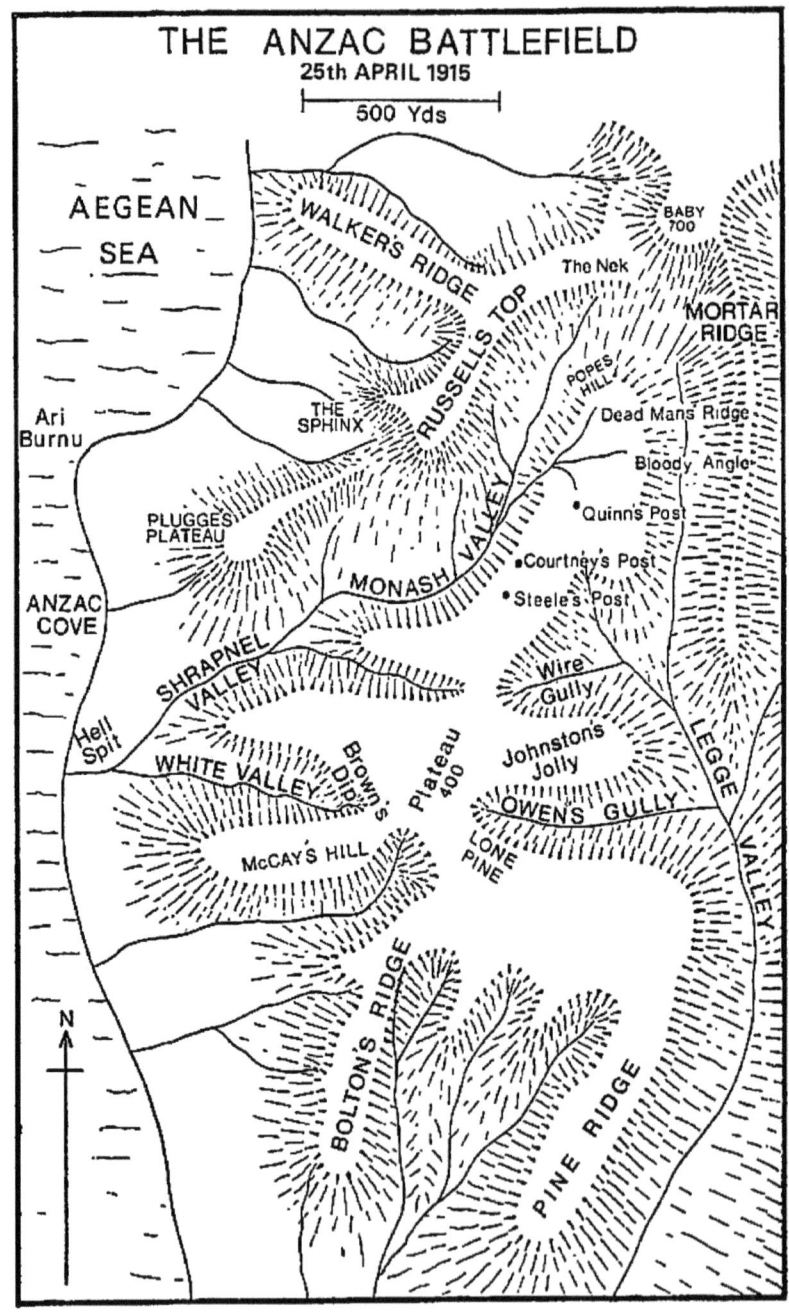

14. The Raid on St Nazaire

27/8 March 1942

You are Lieutenant Colonel Charles Newman[31], the commanding officer of the raid.

Historical Background

DURING WORLD WAR II a British commando and Naval raiding party attempted to block the German-held port of St Nazaire, which had the only dock outside Germany large enough to accommodate the two great German battleships *Bismarck* and *Tirpitz;* the intention was to prevent the Germans forming an Atlantic raiding force based on St Nazaire and Brest. Because of its importance, St Nazaire was well defended with coastal and dual-purpose anti-aircraft guns, plus a garrison of 3-4,000. The six miles of river approach were negotiated by the attacking vessels moving, at high tide, over the sandbanks in the middle of the estuary. The air raid laid on for forty minutes before the actual assault, to divert attention, was not pressed home because of low cloud, but it alerted the defenders.

Friendly Forces
The attacking force consisted of 280 commandos (largely No. 2 Commando) and 350 naval personnel carried in the destroyer *Campbeltown,* 16 motor launches, a motor torpedo boat and a motor gunboat.

Enemy Forces
Unknown

Construction of the terrain

It is not one that can be knocked up in an odd hour before the game starts, because it requires buildings, docks, etc. The dock area can be chalked out on a wargames table or represented by a sheet of card, hardboard or plywood, with the outlines of the docks and jetties, etc, either cut out or marked in. The buildings can be made from card or blocks of wood; or there are excellent card or plastic kits of factories and buildings used in model railway construction[32]. The destroyer

---

[31] Augustus Charles Newman (born 19th August 1904), Lieutenant-Colonel in the Essex Regiment (Territorial Army) was attached to No 2 Commando during the Second World War.

[32] See, for example, Superquick card buildings at www.superquick.co.uk/

Campbeltown, or destroyers like her, exist as kits; the other vessels can be scratch-built, made up from kits or card, or hardboard shapes can be used. The soldiers themselves are cheaply and readily available from sets put out by Airfix.

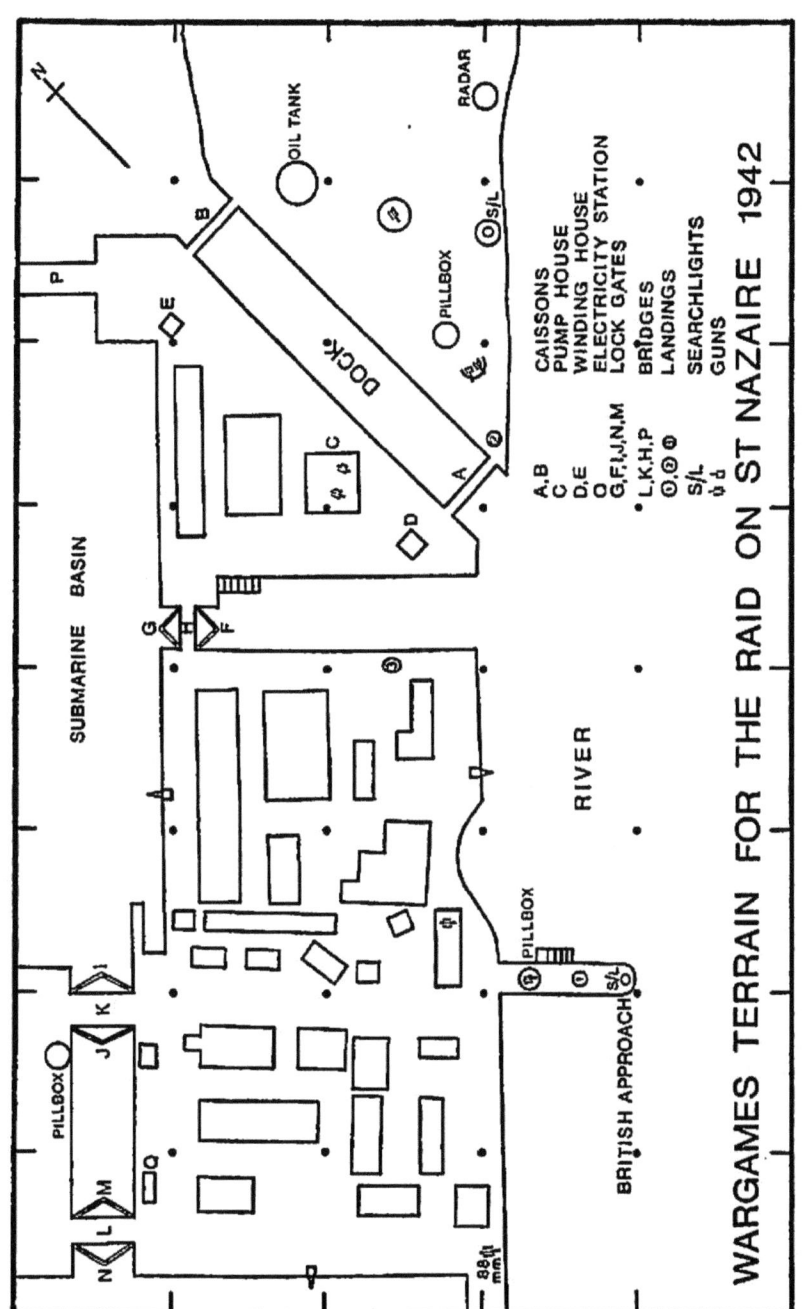

Stop! Read no further until you have deployed the forces and issued your detailed written orders.

The course of the actual historical battle.
In the early hours of the morning of 28th March the attacking force made its way unobserved up the estuary to within less than two miles of the objective, when it was illuminated by searchlights. False radio signals sent out in German won a few minutes' delay, enabling the *Campbeltown* to pass the last point at which she could be fired on by the main coast batteries, so that she was exposed only to the fire of light weapons for the last five or six minutes of the run in. When the enemy's guns opened fire, all the guns on the attacking vessels replied. The *Campbeltown* moved at top speed to break through the torpedo net guarding the lock gate (of the Forme Ecluse) and crash into it with her bows stuck fast as she was scuttled and sank.

The assaulting groups were divided into Headquarters, Assault, Protection and Demolition parties, with a Special Task party and a reserve of twelve men. The job of the assault parties of two officers and twelve other ranks each, armed with Tommy-guns, Brens and rifles, was to form a bridgehead and perimeter, blocking all lines of approach from the main town; to clear the enemy from the outer harbour and destroy the guns there; eliminate the gun positions on each side of the main drydock entrance; to put the guns on the roof of the pumping station out of action; and to destroy the flak towers at the north end of the dock. The Special Task party was to destroy two guns between the Old Mole and the Old Entrance and to damage any ships they came across. The protection parties, armed like the assault parties, and consisting of one officer and four men each, were to guard the demolition parties, whose strength varied according to their task (their only personal arms were revolvers). Their role was to place charges below water level at the main gate to ensure its destruction after it had been rammed by the *Campbeltown,* to blow up the pumping station, to destroy both winding houses and to smash the inner drydock gate—if successful this would put the great drydock out of action for months. Then with only one and a half hours for their task, if time and circumstances permitted, they were to blow up the bridge connecting the dock area with the mainland and, when the troops had withdrawn to the Old Mole (the place of reembarkation), to blow the bridge and dock gates connecting the Old Entrance with the Bassin St Nazaire to prevent any counterattack from making contact and also to make the entrance impossible for U-boats. Finally, the two bridges and sets of dock gates and the lock connecting the outer harbour with the Bassin St Nazaire were to be destroyed.

All but one of the seven motor launches whose job was to land troops on the Old Mole were destroyed or disabled before they could do so. Of the six ML's that were to land their troops at the Old Entrance, one did so, and two others missed the entrance but regained their bearings, and turned to land their commandos. The remaining three ML's in this column were hit before landing their troops.

As soon as the *Campbeltown* struck, Colonel Newman, the Commanding Officer, and his party went ashore at the Old Entrance from motor gunboat 314, and made straight for the point selected as

Headquarters, where they were to meet another party—which did not arrive. Soon the small group was under heavy fire, but was relieved by the arrival of a small group with a 2-inch mortar, which temporarily silenced the guns on the submarine pens.

That part of the force put ashore at the Old Mole encountered heavy and stubborn opposition from two defended pillboxes (which were never completely put out of action), from guns in a high building near the submarine pens, and from machine-guns mounted on the roofs of buildings. Heavy explosions indicated that the demolition parties were carrying out their tasks, although opposition was heavy and considerable fighting took place.

The commando group that went ashore from the *Campbeltown*, organised in a HQ and four parties, had a number of men wounded before getting ashore, but completed all its tasks successfully within the allotted time. Then it withdrew as planned to the bridge over the Old Entrance where, in due course, it was joined by the survivors of the parties which had got ashore at the Old Entrance and the Old Mole.

It was obviously impossible to disembark from the Old Mole, so Colonel Newman and about fifty men, many slightly wounded, after grouping at Headquarters, split up and tried to make their way through the town into the open country, intending to return to England through France and Spain. In the event the majority of them, including Newman (who was awarded the VC), were captured.

HMS Campbeltown blew up at 10.30 am, shattering the dock gate and so damaging the dock that it was never repaired by the Germans.

The British casualties were 144 killed or missing and 215 taken prisoner. The German casualties are believed to have been about 70 killed and an unknown number of wounded.

The battle can begin by involving only those troops who disembarked, accepting that those on vessels known to have been sunk took no part in the simulation. Another way is for the raiding force to be marked on the map at a specified point in the river, and then proceed, with vessels taking casualties from fire as they near the objective. Military Possibilities and Chance Cards can recreate the historical situation, in which the German coastal batteries opened up very late, so allowing the force to get inshore.

The targets of the original raid are listed, but the inclusion of all of them in the table-top reconstruction will be impossible. The targets chosen will be named on the commandos' map and the prime objective will be to destroy them within a specified time. The fate of the raiding party is a secondary consideration, nor is there any value in killing large numbers of Germans.

The 3-4,000 German soldiers were obviously not all in the immediate area of the docks at the onset of the raid; though sentries must have been on duty, pillboxes and other defence posts manned, and coastal batteries and flak towers obviously alerted by the earher air raid, or from the moment firing first began in the river. Therefore, these posts can be manned by adequate numbers of Germans, while the remainder of the force is considered to be 'in barracks' somewhere in the town, so that, once alarmed, it will have to be assembled and transported to the area of fighting. On a Time Chart mark:

(a) the time at which the alarm reached them,

(b) delay while they are rising, dressing, arming themselves and forming up, and

(c) the time taken to embus or proceed on foot to the dock area, considered to be the German 'baseline'.

Up to that point the Germans will be moving 'on paper', and they will only manoeuvre tactically, and as figures on the table, when coming forward from their baseline.

This aspect of the battle can be simulated by having a German 'controller' in another room, with an accurate scale map of the area, a Time Chart and a scaled table of movement. Fed with notes sent back from the points of conflict, he will act by sending troops wherever required.

Outline of the enemy's orders.

Harbour defence companies provide the local security for ships and installations. The 33rd Infantry Division was the local German Army unit; with no troops in the town, several companies were in villages nearby.

There are three pillboxes and a large number of gun positions. Roll a die for each position: 1, 2 or 3 the position is manned and ready; 5 or 6 the position is empty. Roll a 4 and the Germans take 2 moves to man the position.

Each move a section of German infantry may arrive on a roll of 1, 2, 3 or 4. However, they need to roll this number each turn to move due to the confusion of the battle.

Ratings of the Commanders and Military Possibilities

Colonel Newman and Commander Ryder, the Naval commander, will be 'above average' and the German commander, who apparently did nothing particularly wrong or inadequate, can be considered as 'average'.

The morale and fighting qualities of the raiders must always be higher than those of the defending Germans for the following reasons:

1. The attackers were selected, specially trained assault troops.
2. The defenders were run-of-the-mill garrison troops, who might even have been low category men invalided from the Russian Front.
3. The attackers had darkness and surprise as their very powerful allies.
4. The defenders were detrimentally affected by the darkness and surprise, which would make them apprehensive and lower their morale and fighting qualities.

These factors should have speeded up the raiders' reactions, so that, in any face-to-face confrontation, they are always assumed to have fired or taken offensive action before the Germans. The reconstruction will end if the raiding party can get a substantial proportion of its number, with wounded etc, taken off from the Old Mole; or at a point where all its possible targets have been eliminated; or when it is so decimated that few if any of the targets can be destroyed.

There is scope in this operation for some ingenious rules concerning the simulation of explosives and their effectiveness; there should be specified time-factors allowing men to be clear of a building before the charge explodes.

The chapter called 'Personalised Wargames' in *Advanced Wargames* sets out a method of carrying out a commando raid similar to this, with the wargamer naming each member of his force.

Figures suitable for Saint Nazaire

2mm

Irregular Miniatures have generic modern infantry that could be painted as British or German troops.

6mm or 1/300 scale

Adler Miniatures has British and German troops.

Heroics and Ros have World War II British and Germans.

Irregular Miniatures have British and German troops.

10/12mm

Miniature Figurines now owned by Caliver Books of Nottingham has British and German troops, but no Commandos.

Pendraken has British – including a Commandos pack – and German troops.

15mm

Essex Miniatures has British and German troops.

Irregular Miniatures have Germans but no British in this scale.

Old Glory has British and Germans.

Peter Pig has British Commandos and early war British and Germans.

20mm

Airfix made British Commandos – although many, such as canoeists, were in poses unsuitable for St Nazaire - and German troops for World War II.

The website www.plasticsoldierreview.com/Index.aspx lists several sets of British Commandos by different manufacturers, and there are, of course, numerous sets depicting almost every type of German soldier of World War II.

Irregular Miniatures have British and German troops.

25/28mm

Foundry Miniatures have British Commandos, Royal Marines and Germans.

Warlord Games/Bolt Action Miniatures have British troops, including Commandos, and Germans.

Wargame Rules suitable for the Raid on St Nazaire

The freewargamerules website lists numerous rules for Second World War
I Ain't Been Shot, Mum (IABSM for short), TOO FAT Lardies,
PBI: Poor Bloody Infantry a short game of WW2 Company level combat, Peter Pig Rules For the Common Man

Further Reading

Army Commandos 1940-45, Mike Chappell, Osprey Elite 64
British Commandos 1940-46, Tim Moreman, Osprey Battle Orders 18
British Motor Gun Boat 1939-45, Angus Konstam, New Vanguard 166
British Motor Torpedo Boat 1939-45, Angus Konstam, Osprey New Vanguard 74
The German Army 1939-45 (1) Blitzkrieg, Nigel Thomas, Osprey Men At Arms 311
German Infantryman (1) 1933-40, David Westwood, Osprey Warrior 59
Infantry Tactics of the Second World War, Stephen Bull & Gordon L. Rottman, Osprey 2008
Operation Chariot: The Raid on St Nazaire, Jon Cooksey, Leo Cooper Ltd, 2004
The Royal Marines 1939-93, Nick van der Bijl, Osprey Elite 57
Saint-Nazaire: Operation Chariot – 1942 – Battleground French Coast, James G. Dorrian, Leo Cooper Ltd., 2006
St Nazaire 1942: The Great Commando Raid, Ken Ford, Osprey Campaign 92
World War II Street-Fighting Tactics, Stephen Bull, Osprey Elite 168

The historical battlefield map

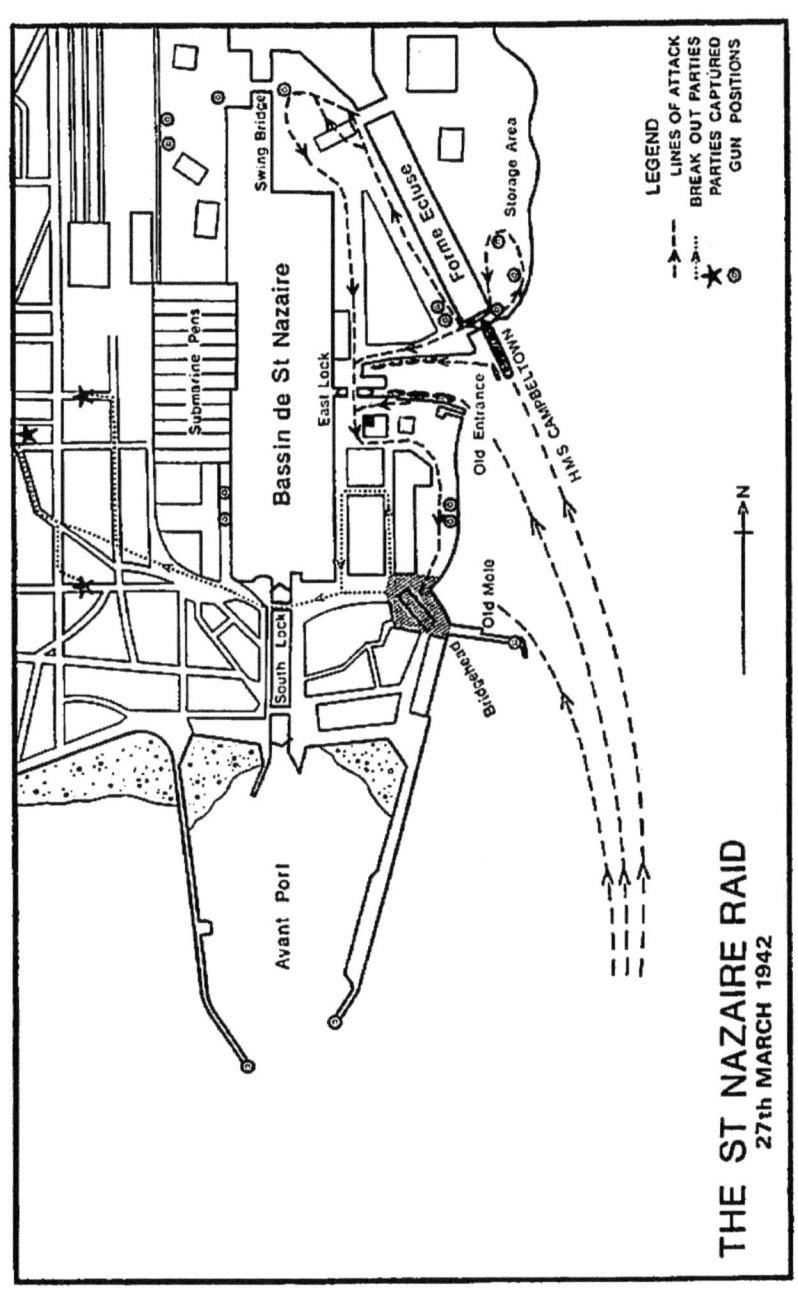

15. The Attack on Pork Chop Hill

16/18 April 1953

You are either 1st Lieutenant Thomas V. Harrold, Company E, 31st Infantry or 1st Lieutenant Joseph G. Clemons Jr.[33], Company K , 31st Infantry.

Historical Background

THIS SMALL-SCALE action was fought between United States infantry and a Chinese Communist force in Korea where, in late 1952 and early 1953, to gain psychological advantages at the Panmunjom Armistice negotiations, the Chinese Communist forces were attempting to overrun UN outposts. Pork Chop Hill, dominated by Chinese-held ridges and inadequately supported by neighbouring positions, was one such outpost. As Vietnam has shown, Korea set the pattern for future wars, with relatively 'soft' soldiers of the Western Democracies battling against hardy fanatical Communist peasants.

Friendly Forces

On the night of the 16th of April Company E, 31st Infantry (1st Lt. Thomas V. Harrold) manned Pork Chop Hill.

17th April at 4.30 am a counter-attack was made by Company K (1st Lt. Joseph G. Clemons, Jr.) and Company L (1st Lt. Forrest J. Crittendon), 31st Infantry

Shortly after the counter-attack began, Company G (1st Lt. Walter B. Russell) 2nd Battalion 17th Infantry arrived to reinforce the counter-attack. Upon reaching the summit, the HQ told the company to withdraw.

21:30 Company F, 17th Infantry (Captain Monroe D. King)

23:00 Company E, 17th infantry (1st Lt. Gorman C. Smith)

---

[33] Joseph Clemons graduated from West Point, where he distinguished himself both and on the athletic field, in 1951 and joined the US Infantry. After completing officer basic training at Fort Benning, Georgia, and an assignment in the 82nd Airborne Division, he reported to A Company, 31st Regiment, 7th Infantry Division in Korea.
There, Lieutenant Clemons heroically led a series of attacks to retake a tactically and strategically critical outpost in the fiercely contested Iron Triangle. His platoon suffered many casualties, but Clemons repeatedly reorganized, rallied, and led his men in ferocious hand-to-hand combat. His courageous leadership earned him the Distinguished Service Cross. Six months later he would be fighting again on similar terrain.

Midnight Company K ordered to withdraw

Enemy Forces

A battalion of the Chinese 201st regiment

Construction of the terrain

As the battle takes place wholly on the hilltop, it can form the entire wargames table as an undulating, cratered and very jumbled terrain. The approach marches by both Americans and Chinese will be carried out on the map, the forces being placed on the table at their points and times of arrival. A sand table is the ideal medium for this terrain, though a satisfactory substitute would be a thick blanket draped over suitable pieces of household impedimenta.

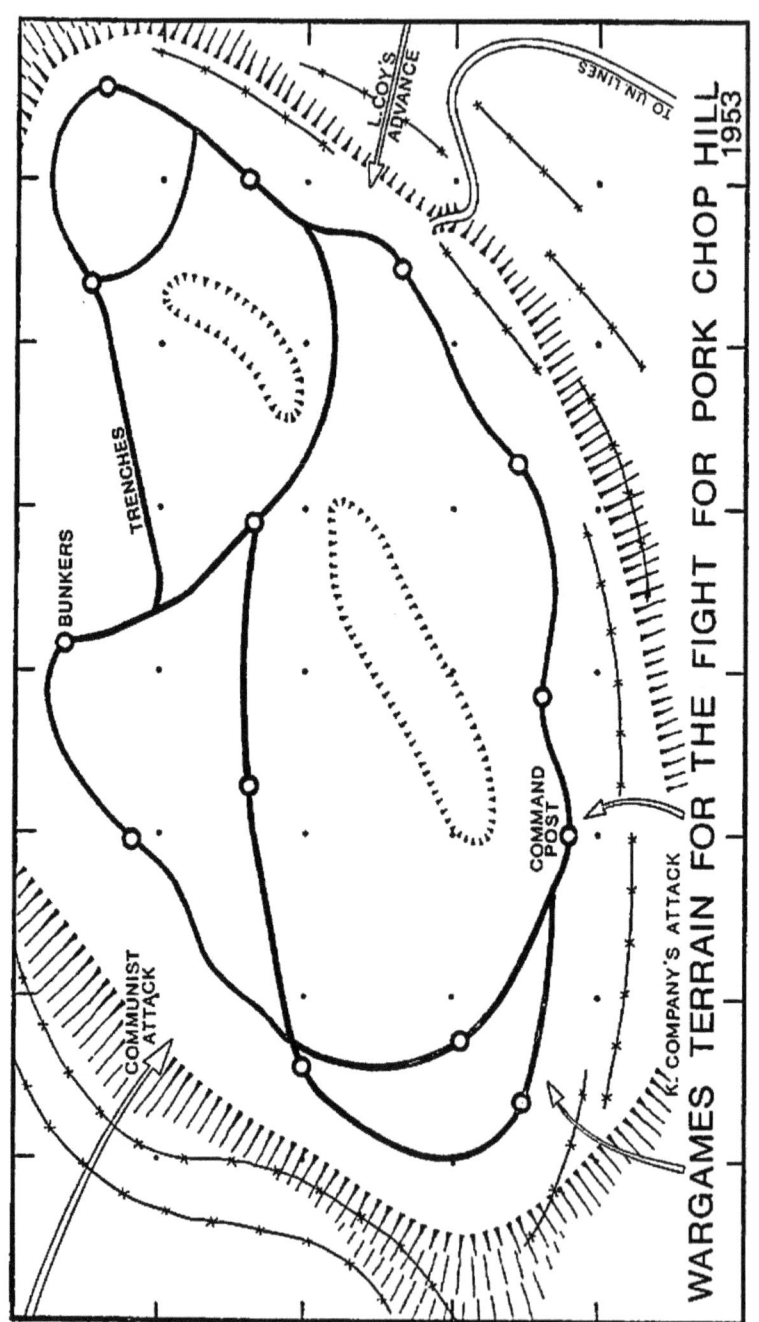

Stop! Read no further until you have deployed the forces and issued your detailed written orders.

The course of the actual historical battle.

On the night of 16 April 1953 Pork Chop Hill was garrisoned by 76 men of the 1st and 3rd Rifle Platoons, Company E, 31st US Infantry Regiment, commanded by Lt T. V. Harrold. Paired-off, 20 GIs and Koreans formed outguards in ten listening posts sited in a crescent around the lower forward and flank slopes. Another group of five men formed half a patrol prowling the small valley forward of the hill. The hilltop itself was encircled by a solidly revetted rifle trench with some roof protection, so that it could be defended against attack from any direction. At thirty yard intervals, loopholed bunkers, sandbagged and heavily timbered, formed part of the trench line. At the rear, the top of the hill was pushed in like the dent in the top of a hat, forming a divided perimeter that forced the two defending rifle platoons into separate compartments, loosely joined in the centre.

Undetected by the outlying patrols, at about 10.30 pm, two companies of CCF infantry, each of about 70 men formed in three platoon columns, crossed the valley almost to the UN position without being seen. When sighted by an outpost, they raced forward and were in the trenches before a shot was fired. Surging like a flood over 1st Platoon's section, they machine-gunned or grenaded the bunkers, killing all but seven of its twenty men. The Communists had hit the position at both ends of 1st Platoon's sector on the left end of the hill and, once in the trenches, they pinched in towards each other.

The Korean confrontation was a conflict fought largely with surplus weapons from World War II, and no startling tactical developments came out of it. By 1953 the best UN soldiers had either been killed or gone home on rotation, and the replacements were green soldiers, unhappy at fighting an unpopular war. The Chinese soldiers, harshly disciplined peasant conscripts, were furtive, fast and skilled, able to move stealthily in the deep valleys and steep hills of Korea. Their night attacks on the heavily defended UN outposts were often successful within minutes. However, they rarely held them under the quickly massed superior fire of American artillery, and the heavy attacks launched by day with artillery, air and armour support.

At 11 pm Lieutenant Harrold fired a red flare signifying that he was under attack and requesting artillery support; and at 11.05 both UN and Chinese guns laid a barrage around the base of the hill. For most of its length on the west side of the hill, where the attack came in, the trench had been covered over with pinewood beams, heaped with sandbags and, in some places, several feet of earth. Crushed in by artillery fire at several points, the fallen roof formed barricades that a rise in the trench-floor turned into successive terraced strongpoints. Here and in other parts of the hilltop position, CCF and American infantry fought with grenades and submachine guns in the maze of trenches and bunkers, but the hill was overrun and, although at dawn the Americans were still holding bunkers and isolated strongholds, for practical purposes the outpost had been lost, since the CCF had gained possession of more than half the hill. Either through exhaustion, fear, the incoming barrage from both UN and CCF artillery, or from insufficient ammunition (carrying little, they relied on captured ammunition), the Chinese infantry squatted in and on the bunkers instead of continuing down the trench line and mopping up.

The defence put up by three officers and four NCO's in the Command Post on the far side of the position from the CCF attack, made the bunker a blockhouse that barred the rear door to the hill, preventing the Chinese from gaining the rear slope and cutting off both line of retreat and route for reinforcements. In the early hours of the morning, two platoons were sent up the hill to reinforce the garrison from F and L Company, but one got lost in the dark and did not arrive, while the other, coming unexpectedly under Chinese fire, ran back into the valley. Then, at 3.30 am Lt Clemons, commanding K Company (135 men), was ordered to assault Pork Chop from its rear while two platoons from L Company went up the hill from the right. K Company riflemen each carried a full belt and bandolier of ammunition for their Garand rifles, and three or more grenades. There were six Browning Automatic Rifles firing five hundred 0.30 rounds per minute with twelve magazines per weapon. Each platoon carried a flamethrower and a 3.5 mm rocket launcher (Bazooka).

K Company advanced up the hill, deploying its 2nd platoon on the right, 1st on the left and 3rd in reserve. From the assault line at the foot of the hill it was only a hundred and seventy yards to the nearest bunkers, but the route was very steep, strung with wire and cratered, with tree stumps and rocky outcrops, so that it took thirty minutes unopposed climbing to reach the top. The Chinese had burrowed into the hill and their artillery doused the area in regular ten minute timed patterns. K Company fought for two hours, becoming exhausted as it gained two hundred yards in a series of individual actions by small groups—all group-initiative having vanished.

The platoons from L Company advancing on a narrow front on the right were mown down by the entrenched defenders so that of the 62 who had attacked under Lt Crittenden, only 10 exhausted men arrived to join Clemons. At 8 am, with both Americans and Chinese out of the trenches and grouped on higher ground inside the *parados*[34], so that they fought at a few feet range, K Company were out of water and short of ammunition. They did not know that the enemy was in a similar position and a determined attack might have recaptured the hill. At about this time, under heavy artillery fire, G Company of the 17th Infantry Regiment, under Lt Russell, struggled up the back slope and joined Clemons, whose force consisted of 35 survivors of K Company, 10 men from L Company and 12 men from Harrold's E Company, rescued from the rubble.

---

[34] *Parados* a French military term for the bank behind a trench or other fortification, giving the occupants protection from being fired on from the rear.

At the same time as G Company was creeping up the cratered slopes, a fresh Chinese company pushed on to the other end of the ridge. The battle suddenly blazed up as men fired and threw grenades amid the jumble of tumbled trenches, shattered bunkers and shell holes, under an almost unceasing artillery fire that fell on the hill. Soon the newly arrived G Company was down to 50 men.

During the early part of 17 April, Clemons was using three Sherman tanks, positioned five hundred yards behind the hill, as artillery to deter the CCF from approaching over low ground west of the hill but, at midday, they obtained permission to depart, fearing that a CCF success on the hill would make them a target for Communist artillery. Then the survivors of G Company were ordered by a misinformed HQ to leave the hill, so at 3 pm Russell had to pull out, leaving Clemons with only 25 men.

While this handful of exhausted men held on to the hill, because the fight was local but the issue national, Division, Corps, Army and Far East Command Headquarters were all debating the simple question: 'Do we really want to hold Pork Chop Hill?' If the hill were yielded, the Communists would strike at another position, but if it were fought for, it might become an attritional trap for battalion after battalion. Finally, the UN accepted that it was going to have to stand up to the CCF or be at a serious disadvantage in the armistice negotiations at Panmunjom, so Lt Denton took L Company on to Pork Chop to join Clemons' remaining 16 men and, at 9 pm F Company mounted the back slopes and relieved demons.

But under the desperate Chinese artillery pounding and infantry attacks, this reinforcement was found to be insufficient, and E Company of the 17th Infantry had to be committed; while at dawn A Company was also sent in as company after company of reinforcing Chinese mounted the hill. Throughout the night and all day of 18 April the UN force, taking 60 and 75 per cent casualties, fought on, until finally the CCF realised that they were not to have the hill, and just after sunset on 18 April the assault ceased as quickly as it began. In his book *Pork Chop Hill* S. L. A. Marshall wrote: 'All the heroism and all of the sacrifice went unreported. So the very fine victory of Pork Chop Hill deserves a description of the Won-Lost Battle. It was won by the troops and lost by the people who had sent them forth.'

Using Airfix or other model soldiers this action can be fought on a man-for-man basis without scaling-down numerical strengths.

Outline of the enemy's orders.

The initial Chinese assault should come from the bottom left hand corner of the table. When the Chinese are in the trenches, they should stop and 'go to ground' without attempting to 'mop up'.

April 18 at 01:30, a second Chinese battalion should assault.

03:20 Further company-sized Chinese assault.

04:20 Further company sized Chinese assault.

Dawn: American Company A, 17th Infantry counter-attacks

Ratings of the Commanders and Military Possibilities

Lt Harrold may be classed as 'average', Lt Clemons as 'above average', and the Chinese commanders as 'average'.

Certainly at the start of the action the CCF would seem to be entitled to a higher morale state, perhaps declining as the action progresses. UN morale is more variable, reflected by local rules that allow the Americans momentarily to break but quickly to recover and fight on. If the Americans are to hold, as they did historically, in spite of the numerical disparity, both sides must be given equal fighting qualities, though at this stage of an unpopular war, with most of the best men gone, it is reasonable to assume that the young American conscripts, fighting in alien territory, were not as effective as their Chinese peasant opponents. Morale differences are balanced by the superior weapons and plentiful ammunition of the Americans. The Chinese, in fact, might well be subject to a Military Possibility that causes them to run out of ammunition and to be unable to find a supply nearby.

At the start of the action E Company is in its defensive positions on and around Pork Chop Hill; both commanders mark their dispositions and movements on a map of the hill and surrounding terrain. Ideally the wargamer representing Lt Harrold, E Company commander, should be unaware of the direction of the CCF attack, which, in fact, reached the position without being seen. The umpire will plot on his master map the progress of the attacking Chinese and whether or not they stumble upon an American/Korean patrol. A Military Possibility can give the American patrols a slight chance of raising the alarm, but the short period of time between the warning and the onslaught will not allow much to be done. The surprise element of the CCF attack can be represented by giving them first fire and imposing a morale penalty on the Americans.

Historically, Lt Harrold called for artillery support, and a Military Possibility (by the use of Chance Cards, etc) can decide whether or not he has time to do this, though the odds should be in his favour. The call for support must be plotted on a Time Chart, which will show that at 11.05 pm the American artillery attempted to seal off the CCF end of the hill, and the Chinese artillery soon tried to do the same at the American end; both sides fire 'off-table map-shoots'. The Time Chart must also plot the gunfire of both sides, which frequently halted the fighting for intervals that must be specified on the Time Chart. During these pauses both sides sheltered in bunkers and in the covered part of the trench. In fact, at about 2 am there were enough Chinese on Pork Chop to mop up and capture it, but the UN and CCF artillery fire prevented them from venturing into the open. These factors must be simulated during the reconstruction. Chinese artillery fired at approximately ten minute intervals almost throughout the entire action; this can be marked on the Time Chart, or the CCF can do a map-shoot at the conclusion of each game-move.

The Chinese soldiers were more at home in the darkness than their American opponents, which advantage may be simulated by throwing a die whenever there is a confrontation between individuals or parties:

4, 5 or 6—the Chinese fire first, 2, 3—the Americans fire first, 1—they fire simultaneously.

Using the Time Chart, bring Clemons and K Company on to the table at the rear of the hill, with the two platoons from L Company coming on the right. If the reconstruction has progressed so as to allow Chinese soldiers to oppose them (in fact, K Company climbed unopposed but L Company took heavy losses) Military Possibilities can determine whether the CCF opposes both, opposes neither, opposes K or L individually, or causes greater or fewer casualties than were caused in the action itself.

Before this, two platoons of F and L Companies had been sent as reinforcements, but neither arrived — a Military Possibility could make one, or both, of them get on to the hill. Similar measures could affect Russell's G Company coming on to the hill and withdrawing at 3 pm, and movements of the various Chinese reinforcing groups. The historical times of these arrivals and departures should be marked on the Time Chart, and then Military Possibilities should be used to ascertain whether they are carried out as they occurred or whether they deviate.

It is recorded history that it was decided to reinforce demons and, if our simulation is to be accurate, this must occur, but Military Possibilities can hasten or slow down the eventual arrival of Lt Denton's L Company, and then F Company and others. The three UN tanks at the foot of the hill could, by a Military Possibility, be called on to the hill by Clemons, where the jumbled terrain would make them extremely vulnerable, though this destroys much of the credibility of the simulation.

This is a highly suitable action for the 'personalised' style of wargaming. Marshall's excellent book includes many of the names of the combatants.

Readers may be interested to know that Captain Joseph Clemons was consultant/advisor on the film *Pork Chop Hill*, starring Gregory Peck, in 1959.

Figures suitable for Pork Chop Hill

2mm

Irregular Miniatures have generic 20th century troops.

6mm or 1/300 scale

Heroics and Ros have American and Japanese World War II figures that could be used.

Irregular Miniatures have World War II US Infantry; suitable figures for Chinese and North Koreans may be found in their WWII Chinese, Japanese and Russian ranges, or in their Vietnam range.

10/12mm

Miniature Figurines now owned by Caliver Books of Nottingham has suitable World War II Americans. North Koreans and Chinese might be converted from Japanese and Russian troops.

15mm

Essex Miniatures has World War II US Infantry but no figures suitable for Koreans.

Old Glory has World War II Americans, Japanese and Russians that could be used.

Peter Pig has WW2 US Marines and Infantry; their Japanese and Russian ranges may contain figures that could pass for North Koreans or Chinese in this scale.

20mm

Readers will find four IMEX sets for the Korean War listed on www.plasticsoldierreview.com/Index.aspx, and suitable American infantry can also be found in the World War II lists. The Pegasus WWII Russian Infantry (Winter Dress) might also provide suitable figures for North Korean or Chinese troops.

Irregular Miniatures have World War II US Infantry that could be used for the Korean War.

Matchlock Miniatures, owned by Caliver Books of Nottingham have a range of metal infantry and offer both North Koreans and Chinese in summer and winter dress.

Wargame Rules suitable for Pork Chop Hill

I Ain't Been Shot, Mum (IABSM for short), TOO FAT Lardies
Krunch-A-Commie: A Game of Combat in the 1950s and 1960s, Milihistriot Quarterly, available on the freewargamesrules website
PBI: Poor Bloody Infantry a short game of WW2 Company level combat, Peter Pig Rules For the Common Man

Further Reading

The Korean War, Carter Malkasian, Osprey Essential History 8
The Korean War 1950-53, Nigel Thomas & Peter Abbott, Osprey Men At Arms 174
On Hallowed Ground: The Last Battle for Pork Chop Hill, Bill McWilliams, Berkley Publishing Group, 2004

US Army Forces in the Korean War 1950-53, Donald Boose, Osprey Battle Orders 11
US World War II and Korean War Field Fortifications 1941-53, Gordon L. Rottman, Osprey Fortress 29

The historical battlefield map

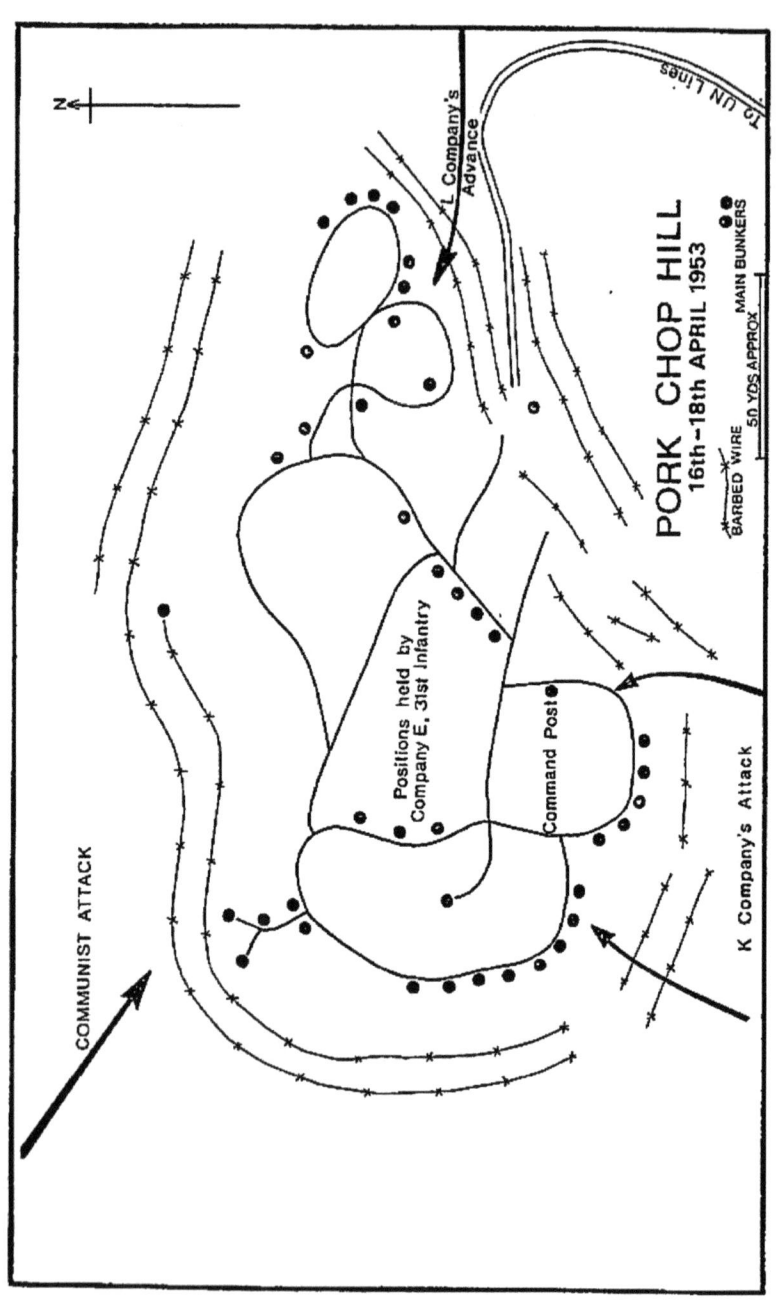

Appendix 1 Rules

RULES ARE principles to which actions or procedures conform or are bound or intended to conform. In wargaming they are based on theory plus the experience and practice of the players themselves who devise them to cover the procedure of their table-top battles, with the intention of bringing to the battle-simulation the greatest possible realism. The majority of readers will have rules of their own that will suffice to control the battles in this book, when supplemented by the suggestions contained in these pages.

There are sets of commercially produced rules, such as those of the Wargames Research Group[35] (75 Ardingly Drive, Goring-by-Sea, Sussex), which publishes a set of Ancient rules 1000 BC to 1000 AD that will cover Pharsalus and Poitiers and probably Barnet; its Horse and Musket Rules 1750-1850 will cover Prestonpans, Maida, Aliwal and perhaps Wilson's Creek; and its Infantry Platoon Action Rules will control the St Nazaire raid and Pork Chop Hill and, at a pinch could be adapted to fit the Gallipoli battle. Cheriton is catered for by the *Musketeer* rules for the period 1490-1690 produced by David Millward[36] (36 Bells Lane, Kings Norton, Birmingham B14 5QN) and English Civil War Rules from D. Featherstone (69 Hill Lane, Southampton SOI 5AD). From the latter source can be obtained sets of Ancient rules that will cover Pharsalus; Mediaeval Rules for Poitiers and Barnet; Eighteenth-Century Rules for Wynendael, Prestonpans and Guilford Courthouse; Napoleonic Rules for Maida; Horse and Musket Rules for Aliwal, Little Big Horn and (with adaptations) Modder River; American Civil War Rules for Wilson's Creek; World War I Rules for Gallipoli; and World War II Rules for St Nazaire and Pork Chop Hill. Maida is also very satisfactorily covered by the Napoleonic Wargames Rules of Stephen and Julian Reed[37] (33 Salvington Hill, High Salvington, Worthing BN13 3BD).

Most historical battles include numerical disparities, surprise factors, varying qualities of troops, inequalities of weapons and morale effects that are extremely difficult to handle under normal wargames rules. For example, the Battle of Aliwal is a particularly good example of a situation where the larger force, both in men and guns, was also protected by field entrenchments, and yet was completely routed by Sir Harry Smith's much smaller army. There are occasions in battle when a commander takes a deliberate calculated risk that no normal

---

[35] The current address of WRG is Suite 260, The Quorum, Barnwell Road, Cambridge CB5 8RE, England. Website: www.wargamesresearchgroup.net Older versions of WRG rules are available on www.freewargamesrules.co.uk

[36] David Millward is now a Director, Webmaster and Programmer for English Computer Wargames, www.wargames.co.uk/ecw/

[37] Published in 1970 and long out of print.

set of wargames rules would allow. Yet the history of warfare demonstrates that many such deviations from the rules are successful, and allowances should be made for breaking the rules on the wargames table.

This leads to the point that local rules are required on the wargames table. It cannot of course be denied that no known set of rules, lacking 'local' adaptations, would give victory to Clive at Plassey, to the British forces in almost any battle of the Indian Mutiny, or in at least half of the battles described in this book. 'Local' rules should therefore make allowances for factors peculiar to a specific battle. No Wargames Rules would allow the 2nd Guards at Guilford Courthouse to recover their morale, for they were completely routed by the 2nd Maryland Regiment and a cavalry attack in their rear, and then heavily hit when Cornwallis ordered his artillery to fire grapeshot into the mêlée. But they rallied in the shelter of the wood, joined the 1st Battalion of Guards and went forward again to the attack. Local rules only can cater for these exceptional incidents.

Eleven out of the fifteen battles herein involve troops of varying qualities, such as Greene's blend of untrained Militia and Continental Regulars at Guilford Courthouse. At least six battles demonstrate marked inequality of weapons and weapon handling, such as the English longbowmen at Poitiers and the American use of flame-throwers on Pork Chop Hill. Distrust of their comrades was shown by the Lancastrians at Barnet and by the Transvaalers at Modder River. The weather played a decisive part at Barnet and, to a certain degree, affected the Cheriton battle; while darkness played a marked role at Prestonpans, Wilson's Creek, St Nazaire and Pork Chop Hill. In no less than twelve battles some or all of the troops were materially affected by morale conditions perhaps peculiar to that conflict. All these factors have to be taken into account if the reconstructions of the battles in this book are to be more than giving names to wargames.

Appendix 2 Terrain

AT LEAST three-quarters of the battles described in this book are vitally affected by the terrain over which they were fought—the positions at Poitiers and Wynendael played a big part in allowing a small force to defeat a numerically superior army; the 'Bloody' lane at Cheriton caused the downfall of the Royalist cavalry; while the maze of gulleys, trenches and mountainous ground caused untold difficulties to the troops at Gallipoli and on Pork Chop Hill.

When attempting to reconstruct any real-life battle, the terrain is perhaps the most important factor in the project because, both in topographical features and dimensions, it must closely resemble the actual battlefield, otherwise what takes place upon it will bear only the most coincidental resemblance to the historical events under simulation.

With three exceptions, the confrontations covered by this book can be constructed within the bounds of a playing surface of 8feet by 5feet. The exceptions are the Little Big Horn, Wilson's Creek and Modder River, where the relatively extensive battle areas lend themselves to division into separate actions, with a coordinated end-result.

When reconstructing a historical battlefield there are two important considerations:
1. It is only necessary to reproduce those areas of the battlefield over which combat took place, so that all possible space on the wargames table can be utilised.
2. Even though it might mean 'ironing out' the known contours of the actual battlefield, all hills and slopes must be so angled as to allow model soldiers to stand up on them.

Perhaps the most realistic wargames terrain is a sand table moulded into hills, valleys, sunken roads, river beds, trenches, shell holes, etc. Sand-table terrains are considered in some detail in my book *Wargames* and my booklet *Wargames Terrain*.

A method of simulating hills, valleys and undulating ground is to stretch a green cloth or plastic sheet over carefully assembled mounds of books, slabs of polystyrene or pieces of wood. Rivers and roads can be painted with poster paint on to the sheeting and look extremely realistic. Slabs of wood or polystyrene placed upon each other to make 'stepped' hills give the terrain a 'symbolic' appearance, providing readily definable contours plus an ideal surface for soldiers to stand upon.

Trees can be made from lichen moss stuck on to pieces of twig; hedges from the same material. Stone walls and rail fencing can be bought or made from balsa wood or plastic ceiling tiles. In fact, these ceiling tiles can be used for houses, bridges, castles, and, when suitably roughened up and painted, make excellent crags and rocky outcrops.

There are innumerable plastic kits of houses, factories, etc, on the market, but the relatively specialised type of buildings required for the St Nazaire terrain may make it necessary for the wargamer to scratch-build.

Although vegetation need not be portrayed on the terrain maps, few stretches of land are completely bald, and the appearance of any battlefield is greatly improved by scattered clumps of trees, bushes and scrub. The terrains of Cheriton, Wynendael and Wilson's Creek had numerous wooded areas. Wargames table woods must be open for troops to manoeuvre without knocking over the trees, so use irregularly shaped pieces of hardboard, painted dark green, with three or four trees around the perimeter.

Bellona[38] Battle Game scenery and landscape models (produced by Micro-Mold Plastic, 1 Unifax, Woods Way, Goring-by-Sea Sussex, England) provide an assortment of earth brown or sand-coloured PVC trenches, sandbagged emplacements, bunkers, ruined buildings, pillboxes, encampments and revetted earthworks. Quickly coloured, the resulting scenic set-pieces are most realistic and effective, and give a professional effect to the terrain.

---

[38] Now no longer in production.

Appendix 3 Website Addresses

To save unnecessary repetition, the current website addresses of manufacturers of wargame figures and publishers of wargame rules listed in the Notes at the end of each chapter are given here, in alphabetic order.

Wargame Figure Manufacturers

Adler Miniatures
    http://home.clara.net/adlermin/
Airfix
    www.airfix.com
Baccus 6mm
    www.baccus6mm.com
Essex Miniatures
    www.essexminiatures.co.uk
Foundry Miniatures
    http://wargamesfoundry.com/
FreiKorp 15
    http://quickreactionforce.co.uk/
Heroics and Ros
    www.heroicsandros.co.uk
Irregular Miniatures
    www.irregularminiatures.co.uk
Magister Militum
    www.magistermilitum.com
Matchlock Miniatures
    www.wargames.co.uk/traders/caliver/matchlock.htm
Miniature Figurines (Minifigs)
    http://miniaturefigurines.co.uk/Home.aspx
Old Glory UK
    www.oldgloryuk.com
Pendraken
    www.pendraken.co.uk
Perry Miniatures
    www.perry-miniatures.com/
Peter Pig
    www.peterpig.co.uk
Wargames Foundry
    http://wargamesfoundry.com/
Warlord Games
    www.warlordgames.co.uk/

Wargame Rule Publishers

Baccus 6mm
   www.baccus6mm.com
Dadi & Piombo
   www.dadiepiombo.com/impetus2.html
Freewargamerules website
   www.freewargamesrules.co.uk/
Junior General website
   www.juniorgeneral.org
Miniature Wargaming website
   www.miniaturewargaming.com/
Osprey/Slitherine
   www.ospreypublishing.com
The Perfect Captain
   http://perfectcaptain.50megs.com/
Peter Pig
   www.peterpig.co.uk
Realistic Modelling Services
   www.realisticmodelling.com/catalog.asp?subrange=rules
TOO FAT Lardies
   http://toofatlardies.co.uk/
Wargames Foundry
   http://wargamesfoundry.com/
Warhammer Historical
   www.warhammer-historical.com/index.html
Warlord Games
   www.warlordgames.co.uk/

Other rules, especially those published in the United States, may be obtained from Caliver Books of Nottingham, www.caliverbooks.com/

Bibliography[39]

IN ADDITION to those listed in the individual chapters, the following may also be consulted:

Dupuy, R E. and T. N. *The Encyclopedia of Military History from 3500 BC to the Present* (1970): Pharsalus, Poitiers, Barnet, Prestonpans, Guilford Courthouse, Maida, Wilson's Creek, Little Big Horn, Modder River, Gallipoli, St Nazaire
Eggenberger, David. *A Dictionary of Battles from 1479 BC to the Present* (1967): Pharsalus, Poitiers, Barnet, Prestonpans, Guilford Courthouse, Maida, Wilson's Creek, Little Big Horn, Modder River, Gallipoli
Kinross, John. *Discovering Battlefields in Southern England* (paperback, nd): Barnet, Cheriton, Prestonpans

PHARSALUS

Hadas, Moses and the Editors of Time-Life Books. *Imperial Rome* (1966)
Montgomery, Field-Marshal Viscount. *A History of Warfare* (1968)
Webster, Graham. *The Roman Imperial Army* (1969)

POITIERS

Bryant, Arthur. *The Age of Chivalry* (1963)
Burne, Alfred H. *The Crecy War* (1955)
Featherstone, D. F. *The Bowmen of England* (1967)
Montgomery, Field-Marshal Viscount. *A History of Warfare* (1968)

BARNET

Barnett, C. R. B. *Battles and Battlefields in England* (1896) Fortescue, Sir John W. *A History of the British Army,* Vol I (1899)
Grant, James. *British Battles on Land and Sea* Vol I (nd)

CHERITON

Adair, John. *Cheriton* (1972)
Godwin, G. N. *The Civil War in Hampshire* (1904)
Rogers, Colonel H. C. B., OBE. *Battles and Generals of the Civil Wars 1642-1651* (1968)

---

[39] The original bibliography, reprinted to show the sources available to the author.

WYNENDAEL

Atkinson, C. T. *Marlborough and the Rise of the British Army* (1921)
Belfield, Eversley. *Oudenarde 1708* (1972)
Fortescue, Sir John W. *History of the British Army*, Vol I (1899)
Grant, James. *British Battles on Land and Sea* (nd)

PRESTONPANS

Fortescue, Sir John W. *History of the British Army*, Vol II (1910)
Tomasson, Katherine and Buist, Francis. *Battles of the '45*, (paperback, 1962)

GUILFORD COURTHOUSE

Fortescue, Sir John W. *History of the British Army*, Vol III (1911)
Reid, Courtland T. *Guilford Courthouse*, National Park Service Historical Handbook Series No 30 (paperback,1959)

MAIDA

Battles of the Nineteenth Century Described by Archibald Forbes, G. A. Henty, Major Arthur Griffiths and Other Well-Known Writers, Vol II (1902)
Fortescue, Sir John W. *History of the British Army*, Vol V

ALIWAL

Battles of the Nineteenth Century, Vol II (1902)
Featherstone, D. F. *All For a Shilling a Day* (1966)
Featherstone, D. F. *At Them With the Bayonet!* (1969)
Fortescue, Sir John W. *History of the British Army*, Vol XII (1934)
Lunt, Sir J. *Charge to Glory* (1962)
Moore-Smith, G. C. *The Autobiography of Sir Harry Smith* (1901)

WILSON'S CREEK

Catton, B. *This Hallowed Ground* (1957)
Commager, H. S. *The Blue and the Grey*, Vol I (1950)
Johnson, R. V. and Buel, C. C. (eds). *Battles and Leaders of the American Civil War*, Vol. I. (1956)
Pratt, F. *Ordeal by Fire* (1950)

LITTLE BIG HORN

Battles of the Nineteenth Century, Vol I (1902)
Luce, Edward S. and Evelyn S. *Custer Battlefield*. Historical Handbook Series, No 1 (paperback, 1949)

MODDER RIVER

Battles of the Nineteenth Century, Vol III (1902)
Pemberton, W. Baring. *Battles of the Boer War* (paperback,1964)
Wilson, H. W. *With the Flag to Pretoria: A History of the Boer War of 1899-1900,* Vol I (1900)

ANZAC LANDING AT GALLIPOLI

Armstrong, H. C. *Grey Wolf* (paperback, 1935)
James, Robert Rhodes. *Gallipoli* (1965) *Soldiers Battle Tales from 'Blackwood's'* (1968)

ST NAZAIRE

St Nazaire Raid, The (Campaign Book), Purnell's History of the 2nd World War (paperback)
Saunders, Hilary St George. *The Green Beret* (paperback, 1949)

PORK CHOP HILL

Fehrenbach, T. R. *This Kind of War* (1963)
Marshall, S. L. A. *Pork Chop Hill* (paperback, 1956)

www.ingramcontent.com/pod-product-compliance
Ingram Content Group UK Ltd.
Pitfield, Milton Keynes, MK11 3LW, UK
UKHW021350250425
5634UKWH00039B/1246